C000193988

GOING DOWN

GOING DOWN

Reflections of a
Reluctant Diver

Amanda Ursell
with Gérald Rambert

NEW
HOLLAND

First published in 2006 by New Holland Publishers (UK) Ltd
London • Cape Town • Sydney • Auckland

10 9 8 7 6 5 4 3 2 1

www.newhollandpublishers.com

Garfield House, 86–88 Edgware Road, London W2 2EA, UK

80 McKenzie Street, Cape Town 8001, South Africa

14 Aquatic Drive, Frenchs Forest, NSW 2086, Australia

218 Lake Road, Northcote, Auckland, New Zealand

Copyright © 2006 in text: Amanda Ursell
Copyright © 2006 in photographs: Gérald Rambert
Copyright © 2006 in artwork: New Holland Publishers (UK) Ltd
Copyright © 2006 New Holland Publishers (UK) Ltd

All rights reserved. No part of this publication may be reproduced, stored in a retrieval
system or transmitted, in any form or by any means, electronic, mechanical,
photocopying, recording or otherwise, without the prior written permission of the
publishers and copyright holders.

ISBN 1 84537 266 2

Publishing Manager: Jo Hemmings
Project Editor: Kate Parker
Design and cover design: Adam Morris
Illustrator: Phil Garner
Production: Joan Woodroffe

Reproduction by Modern Age Repro Co. Ltd, Hong Kong
Printed and bound by Replika Press Pvt. Ltd, India

Publisher's Note: The author and publishers have made every effort to ensure that the
information contained in this book is correct at the time of going to press, and they
accept no responsibility for any loss, injury or inconvenience sustained by any person
through using this book.

For ML

Dum spiro (compressed air or otherwise) ti amo

CONTENTS

Prologue

When do we ever get the chance these days to escape from the infernal bleeping of our text messages, the ring of the phone, the blare of the telly and the general buzz of contemporary life? The tranquillity seemed surreal. I've never really 'heard' myself breathe before except when panting and out of breath running for the bus, but underwater with the scuba gear it seemed that every slow inhalation and exhalation was audible, letting you know that you were alive and well, even though present in someone else's world – the world of fish and coral, sea plants and wonderful submarine rock formations usually hidden from the human eye. I struggled to find an occasion I could remember when I'd 'heard' such quietness. No cars, sirens, planes. No buzzing soundtrack of day-to-day living. Scuba-diving, it seemed, offered the chance to once again capture some silence. Some 'me' time. Some time to contemplate and reflect. Time to wind down and simply glide and look. And to feel, see and absorb the peace.

CHAPTER 1

No way, José

'Me? Scuba-dive? You must be joking!' I replied to my friend Roz, warmly tucked up and idly tracing patterns on the cappuccino froth in my favourite café on King's Road, London SW3.

'Well, you're off to the Indian Ocean – I thought you might give it a whirl,' she ventured.

'I'm hydro-, claustro- and sharkophobic,' I said, suddenly dropping my teaspoon and gulping down mouthfuls of caffeine. 'I don't like the sea, small places or the idea of being breakfast for a great white. So absolutely not. Not in a million years . . . but thanks for asking.'

I don't know anything that I've ever been so sure about: the thought of scuba-diving has, quite simply, always given me the willies. And so, just three days later, when the Head of Public Relations at our lovely hotel in Mauritius, where I was working on a television show, repeated Roz's question, my obvious response was, without hesitation, 'No thanks'.

Like many people, I really do have a thing about feeling closed in. It may not actually be fully fledged claustrophobia, but I'm the sort who insists on sitting at the end of the row in the cinema, from where I have a clear run to the exit, and who would rather walk on hot coals than face being crammed in with hundreds of sweaty bodies on the London Underground. Lifts? Forget them. I'd prefer to be found conked out from exhaustion in a stairwell than get stuck in a metal box transporting people between floors.

As for the hydro-, sharkophobic business, well, ever since my dad told my childhood best friend Jane and me, both aged nine and floating on a lilo off the coast of Aldwick, near Bognor Regis, that there were sharks in the English Channel (he meant 'basking', we understood 'man-eaters'), I've barely put so much as a big toe into saline water of any description. Who knows what could be lurking beneath the waves?

Meeting Gérald

This was why scuba-diving seemed out of the question. Until – and of course there has to be an 'until' otherwise I wouldn't be writing this book – one particular instructor, Gérald, of Sun Divers centre in Flic en Flac, off the west coast of Mauritius, gently, actually, almost without me realising, nudged me towards having a go. It was his photographs that clinched the deal. A sort of modern-day 'Would you like to see my etchings?' approach to tempting people into places they would normally never go. Imagine some of Versace's wilder creations. Throw in a little of the drama of the costumes of the 16th-century French court and then times it by 100. That is how the extraordinary, multicoloured, other-worldly creatures that he zapped past my astonished eyes on the screen of his computer appeared to me.

There were fish that appeared like over-dressed Indian emperors and some that looked for all the world like massive great stones. Others were striped like tigers. I saw sea slugs that seemed like tiny, highly decorated space ships having docked on a nearby rock and eels that, far from eating the crustaceans precariously perched on their mouths, were actually enjoying morning ablutions performed by these busy little cleaner prawns.

It was then, staring at the screen in utter bewilderment and disbelief, that I suddenly realised I just had to see these for myself to believe they were real. I mean, maybe he had photoshopped them – you never know these days. But perhaps most of all, even more than wanting the evidence first hand that someone or something had been able to create such an incredible world of underwater creatures, I wanted to experience and 'feel' the peace and serenity that his photography and film clips had captured.

In-built fears

But back to the real world. How on earth does one get from the comfy viewing of computer images to being in that place of solitude? There remained those substantial hurdles to cross. How do you overcome fears that have been with you since your earliest memories? Personally, I began my journey from sun lounge lizard to tentative snorkelling by chatting with my good friend, life coach Pete Cohen, who, rather fortuitously, was working on the same television show in Mauritius and who gave me 20 minutes of his time to explain the root of our so-called 'in-built' fears. He asked me if I had been born with my fears.

'Born with them? What do you mean?'

'Well,' said Pete, 'did you pop out into the world and the first thoughts you ever had were of fearing the sea, large fish and small spaces?'

Of course the answer was I hadn't.

'We learn our fears,' explained Pete, 'we pick them up from society and people around us and then we just play them out in our everyday lives. How many times have you heard people say "Oh, I'm so scared of spiders" and go completely frantic when they spy even the tiniest little eight-legged creature scuttle across the floor?'

Good point. If you think about it, spiders in the UK are not that scary. I mean, being frightened to death of waking up and finding a redback crawling across your chest if you live in Australia is a very rational fear. In Europe, it just simply isn't going to happen. OK, the odd dangerous specimen may make it through Customs buried in a bunch of bananas,

but in everyday life, being scared of spiders is a knee-jerk reaction that we learn from those around us.

I've never actually had a problem with the eight-legged scuttlers myself, and that attitude I put down completely to seeing my lovely grandma deal with even the biggest, most hairy specimens you can imagine by scooping them gently and lovingly up in her duster and cooing things like 'Come on you sweetheart, back out to where you belong,' while shaking them with great care out of the window.

Pete explained that all you have to do is to unlearn your fears. The truth is I know, logically, that this is possible. I have seen Pete, within a very short space of time, help people with a fear of heights feel more than comfy being hoisted into the air in a fireman's basket to get a bird's eye view of the world. I've seen him deal with those quite literally petrified of snakes so they end up handling socking great boa constrictors. I know you can face your fears and conquer them because I've seen it happen to others with my own eyes.

I remember my reaction to Pete telling me more about this as we lazed on the beach with a coconut cocktail. On the whole, he said, it comes down to having the guts to change your point of view. Give things a go and see if you are *really* scared or if you just *think* you are scared. It is all a question of smashing your limiting beliefs to pieces.

'Limiting beliefs? What are they then?' I asked.

'All the things that limit you from doing what you can really do, that limit you from being the person you can be,' said Pete, as he took a slurp.

Hmm. I wanted to see these fish. I wanted to feel the peace. The only things stopping me were fears that had become so ingrained in my brain they had become real.

It seemed that the only thing to do was to prove to myself that they weren't. And the starting place was to put on a snorkel.

OK, confession time: I *had* snorkelled as a small child in Spain, off the edge of pedalo boats with my dad, brother and cousins, a good three years before the 'lilo' day. Goodness knows how, but I'd actually managed to forget this fact somehow. But it all came back. Before seeing *Jaws*, before those seeds of fear of the deep blue ocean had been planted in my brain, my family and I had dived down with fins to collect shells and – oh my goodness – to look at the fish. I found it hard to believe that I could have forgotten those early childhood experiences. The power of the mind is that strong.

Taking the plunge

I slept on Pete's words and those resurrected memories, and the next day crept down to the beach. The first step was to get into the flipping sea and have a swim. Snorkels and masks would have to wait. Treading on a flat fish wasn't a good start. My cartoon-style fleeing back to the shore must have looked ridiculous. But back into the water I went. OK, it was only a 5-minute plunge and the depth was about, oh, half a metre but it was a start.

The next step was to borrow a snorkel. Instead of scary thoughts like 'I've seen killer whales on *Blue Planet* leap onto beaches to grab innocent seals for a quick snack,' I tried to imagine those times in Spain. 'Put the flipping mask on,' said one side of the brain, 'top up your tan, go back to the sun lounger,' said the other. Since the latter is supposed to give you skin cancer, it seemed both had their pros and cons.

At this point, I think it's important to say when I chatted with my friend Alexander, a psychologist, about this 'overcoming your fears' stuff, he warned me: 'Don't make it seem like everyone can do this, Amanda. It is true, most people can take this approach, but there are some for whom pushing their personal comfort boundaries is not sensible.' I guess you have to know yourself well enough to make this judgement. As Alexander says, scuba-diving isn't for everyone, and however much I yap on about it, you must listen to your own inner voice. If it says an out-and-out, definitive 'No', then it is better not to go for it.

With a little help from my friends

When confronting one's fears it is wise to enlist the help of others. Going it alone is sometimes really not an option. Enter my mate Nicki, also filming in Mauritius. Nicki isn't scared of anything. When she water-skis she thinks of the fantastic time she's having, not that she's going to fall off. When skiing she heads for the black runs, and (she must be out of her mind) she wants to take up kite-boarding. She is mad, but just the type you need for a snorkelling trip out on a boat, beyond the safety of the reef where the bottom of the sea is a tad more than an arm's length away.

If you haven't snorkelled before, it does feel a bit weird putting the mouthpiece in your mouth, so it's sensible to take the time to find one that fits. If it's too big you feel like a wide-mouthed frog; if it's too small it keeps popping out. The idea is that once it's in place, you bite gently so that your lips create a seal around the rubber. Doing this also helps to hold the snorkel in place. Then you need to blow out first, to clear any water that might be in the tube part so that you don't inhale it and splutter and panic like mad. This is good practice for when you are in the sea: water inevitably splashes in and it needs to be given a good blow to get it out. If you dive down a bit, then it completely fills up and to flush this out once you are back at the surface you need to give a really strong blast a couple of times.

You also need to get used to just breathing through your mouth since your nose is encased within the mask. I once saw a friend of mine practise on the beach. He looked a bit peculiar wearing his mask and snorkel while sitting on the sand, but hey, he mastered the breathing that way and insists it's the way to learn. When you are actually swimming along at the surface of the sea with your snorkel and mask in place, the idea is to breathe slowly and quite deeply. As you get used to it, the gentle rhythm of slow breaths takes over and you stop thinking about it – especially if you are lucky enough to spot some interesting marine life.

My first trip out in the boat was with Fred, who ran the boathouse at the hotel, Nicki, and some other snorkellers who were oblivious to any anxiety on my part. It wasn't all plain sailing. First, I didn't want to leave the boat. We seemed to be absolutely miles out and, as I peered over the edge, I definitely couldn't see the bottom. Fred and Nicki were brilliant, but I was, in spite of Pete's words, still carrying quite a bit of fear. Eventually the 'I can do this' side of my brain took over and I made myself go in. I did enjoy it … a little bit … but I was still anxious. Not because of the technical snorkelling bit, but just because I still found the sea a bit scary. When the time came to head back to the boat, as far as I was concerned, it couldn't have been soon enough. Even so, I'd made the point to myself: I could do it. It wasn't easy; most of it hadn't even been that much fun; but, and here's the but, I had caught enough of a glimpse of some fascinating fish to want to do it again, and to get closer to them. To see them eye to eye, not as a voyeur peering down from the surface. And that, of course, meant one thing: I'd have to give scuba-diving a whirl. Mastering the snorkel was, it turned out, a step in the right direction, since part of the clobber that comes with getting yourself kitted out for scuba-diving includes the simple snorkel.

A family affair

Seeing the pretty fish and feeling the tranquillity of the underwater world may not be sufficient motivation to get everyone snorkelling, let alone to see them taking the next step towards the fully submerged tank-on-the-back stuff. Some want to give a go for the sake of their loved ones. This seems to be a good reason for many. It certainly was for Debs. I met Debs while sitting at the bar of La Pirogue hotel in Flic en Flac, Mauritius, one day. She was looking longingly at a dive boat as it swept away from the shore with her entire family on board, off for their morning dive.

'God, I'd love to be with them,' she murmured from under her sun hat. 'They absolutely love it and I would never stop them going … but I do get lonely whiling away the hours alone here each day. It's not just the time the diving takes, it's the fact that I can't join in the conversation for the next couple of hours when they get back. I just wish I had the nerve to do it too. I guess at 45 I'm never going to now. The whole thing scares me silly. The claustrophobia—'

Here we go, I thought, I know what's coming next: sharks and the deep water. Sure enough, sharks and the deep water it was. It was one year later that I saw Debs again, mask in one hand, fins in the other and a massive grin on her face. 'You're never going to believe this!' Well, you know what's coming next. She got home to Italy and the sheer boredom of family holidays got the better of her. She secretly signed up for scuba lessons and, to the astonishment of her husband and three children, the following year joined them on the boat, consigning her coffee days at the bar to a caffeine-drenched past.

Others take a more masterful approach to the non-diving spouse: 'I just got completely fed up with my wife sitting at the breakfast table before I left for my dive sighing deeply and asking "When will you be back?"' said a diver one morning. 'To be honest, it got to breaking point a couple of years into our marriage. Either I would have to give up diving or my clock-watching wife was going to have to join me. She's not the sporty type, so she assumed she wouldn't like it, but after I bought her some lessons she promised to at least have a try dive. We agreed that if she hated it that would be fine. I'd never utter another word and my American Express card was all hers while I went off diving. Well, talk about a fish to water. Now it costs me more keeping her in scuba gear than it would if she were hitting the local shopping centre with my credit card doing its flexible thing.'

That struck me as a slightly overly manful approach. I loathe being put in a corner about anything, but horses for courses, and it worked for them. Personally I'd have left him, but it takes all sorts, and I'm glad that she got her own back by splurging out on the gear!

The age barrier

Then there was Maddie from Germany. She and her husband were diving nuts. Every day of every holiday they were out there doing two dives a day and with them, much to my astonishment, was Maddie's 72-year-old father Hans. Hiding emotions has never been my forte and the 'Crikey, isn't he a bit on the old side?' expression that obviously flashed across my face when I saw Hans board the boat clearly having every intention to dive was enough to elicit a quiet word in my ear.

'He took it up when he was 65,' Maddie whispered. 'We regaled him with so many tales of the wonders of the deep that he bought some diving books, had a medical and off he went. He loves it. The only thing he complains about is having to have the doctor's once-over every time he dives! He's always been fit, but his determination to keep diving has really given him the incentive to maintain his workouts, regular walking and weight training, which I think is excellent.'

There is no doubt that under normal circumstances, as we get older, our lungs become less effective, our arteries stiffen and we lose some of our strength. All negatives when it comes to scuba diving. But the good news is that if, like Maddie's dad, you can reduce these natural declines and the fancy takes you, you can still take up scuba diving at an age when others are thinking about their cocoa and slippers.

At the other end of the age spectrum, the best advice when it comes to children learning to dive is to never, ever push them into it. If they are reluctant, then listen to them. Children need to be physically and psychologically mature enough to cope with diving. Different training organisations have slightly different recommendations regarding the age at which youngsters can start to scuba dive, but the golden rule is: whatever the official age is set at, kids are one group you should never cajole. Let the desire to dive come 100 per cent from them.

From shopping trolleys to coral

For Mat and Maz, fantastic friends I met on one of several trips to Mauritius, the motivation to dive was simple. Some day they want to take off and open their own dive centre, preferably somewhere hot with beautiful warm water. In order to achieve this goal they took what I can now see is quite a sensible option. They did their initial training in the UK.

'It was in a gravel pit in Kent,' explained Mat. 'We absolutely froze our nuts off, but it meant that once we got here we could take straight to the sea and get stuck in.' Any reluctance on their part caused by the seriously low water temperatures was overcome by wanting to achieve their future goal.

One good thing about doing their training back at home, was that when they reached Mauritius, the fish took them as much by surprise and inspired them as much as Gérald's photographs had me. It took just one dive in the crystal clear seas to know that they had made the right career choice when they braved those cold winter mornings in Kent.

'We were used to seeing about a foot in front of us in the gravel pit and the most interesting things we saw were the odd shopping trolley and old double decker bus. Being able to see for miles in front and to be surrounded by the amazing marine life is awesome.'

It seems that there is a myriad of reasons for people to have a go at scuba diving and like me, not everyone begins with a life-long burning passion. For many, though, it becomes one.

CHAPTER 2

From snorkelling to swimming pool: Lesson one

Lesson one in scuba-diving (after learning that 'SCUBA' stands for Self-contained Underwater Breathing Apparatus) is that there is a huge amount of clobber that goes with this 'sport', and you get your first feel of it during your practice sessions in the pool or wherever your path to scuba-diving begins. This may be a European lake, the shallow waters of a tropical island or in your local swimming pool near home. Wherever the venue for your first underwater foray, one thing is for sure: there is no escaping the gear that on land makes you feel like the most ungainly person alive.

I guess it's only natural. I mean, Neil Armstrong wasn't shot into space in his birthday suit. To breathe in space and to survive the unnatural conditions of the outer atmosphere, he was kitted up to the hilt. The good news for divers is that at least you don't need a spacecraft and the gear is nothing like as cumbersome as that of astronauts. Also, it's progressed beyond all recognition when compared to the first intrepid divers in the 19th century, who took to the deep with heavy metal helmets and bits of tubing to the surface that provided the air.

I was reading all about this recently in *The Infernal Diver* by well-known technical diving writer and historian Dr John Bevan. Really, those divers were either absolutely stark, staring nuts or unbelievably brave, in my view. Actually, probably both. Those men (they were all men in those days) ventured into the deep in contraptions that defy belief. And it is they we can thank for playing their role in ensuring that, although hardly lightweight, the equipment today is as streamlined and safe as it is.

Kitted out

Here we go, from top to bottom: first, there is the mask to cover your eyes and nose, because obviously you are going to want to see when underwater. Next, there is the rubber mouthpiece, which is connected to your tank via rubber tubing to supply your air, and a sleeveless jacket-type affair that you put on like a waistcoat and do up at the front. On the back of this is attached the rather heavy tank containing that vital air. Moving on down you get to your flippers, although you get a real telling-off if you call them this, because the real word for them is 'fins'.

Of course, practically everywhere you dive, even if the water is really warm, you normally wear a wetsuit, even if only for protection from getting scratched by rocks and stung by things you would rather not be stung by. More on that later. The thickness of the suit depends on the temperature of the water in which you are diving. For warmish waters there are different thicknesses of wetsuits, but in really chilly waters like those around the coasts of England, Ireland and Scotland, most people agree that a dry suit is needed instead, inside of which you can wear duvet-like undersuits to warm off the perishing temperatures into which you submerge yourself.

Very few people, with the exception of supermodels and skinny men, look good in wetsuits. It is a sad fact, but one that it is best to grasp early on. However snazzy your particular suit looked hanging up in the dive centre or in a photo in a magazine, yours won't be the same once you have grappled and tugged, cussed and yanked it on. The best advice is not to look in a mirror and not to have your photo taken, unless it is from the waist up. Otherwise, vanity alone may prevent you from ever making it to the pool session.

In the pool

Once you have made it to the location of your first lesson and have finally got into all of this gear, it is time to get down to the business of learning the basics. The good news is that once you are actually in the water you no longer feel or look like an oversized, waddling penguin. All of the paraphernalia begins to make sense and no longer weighs you down like a lead balloon as it does on land.

My instructor Gérald began by getting me to put the mask on, to pop the regulator in my mouth and, one, two, three, to put my head under and take my first actual sub-aquatic breaths. Did I like it? No. Was it in any way enjoyable? No. It was claustrophobic and I wanted to yank the gear off and get back to the café for a soothing cuppa as quickly as possible. The fact that when I came up for some real air, the others with me were completely fine, heads still underwater and breathing away merrily and safely, made me give it another go. A touch of personal pride had set in, and thank goodness for that. An element of 'If they can, I can' came into play and this helped put Pete's 'change your point of view' malarkey into practice.

That, and the motivation to see the fish close up and to experience the peace underwater, was sufficient to make me try to talk myself round. 'OK, OK, change your point of view,' I muttered. 'The pool is big, I'm not enclosed, the air supply is working and I can scarper if I want to … but I don't want to. I want to blinking well do this.' So under I went. The key, it seems to me, is to stop flapping, because then your breathing slows down and then, yes, you can hear your breaths. 'Oh my gawd, I'm doing it! It's OK!' I wanted to yell, although of course you can't since the rubber thing in your mouth makes chatting impossible. Next step: feet off the bottom and swim, just like a fish. 'Yippee! It's OK. I'm breathing, I'm swimming, and I'm changing my point of view, Pete!!'

BANG! Straight into the instructor. Amid the excitement,

From snorkelling to swimming pool **25**

I'd forgotten to look where I was going. One panic and I was gasping for air at the surface again. It immediately became apparent that scuba-diving is not a sport to get over-confident in. It soon brings you back to reality with a bump. It wasn't a bad bump though. Hurdle Number One was definitely over.

Learning to breathe air, not water

Now it was on to some of the more technical stuff. The next thing to achieve in the pool it appeared, was taking your mouthpiece (it's actually called the 'regulator' I discovered at this point) out of your mouth while underwater, and then replacing it. When you take it out of your mouth, obviously, the regulator fills up with water, so when you put it back in, if you breathe straight away, you gulp down water not air. Not very nice and a sure-fire way to up the odds of drowning yourself. The idea with this exercise is to take out the regulator, deliberately allow it to fill with water, put it back into your mouth and then to either breathe out and push the water out that way, or to press a button of the front of the regulator that flushes the water out and then lets you breathe again.

It doesn't sound complex, but this weird thing happened to my brain when I was underwater on the first few occasions. I imagine it's a bit like being on *Who Wants to Be a Millionaire* with Chris Tarrant asking, for £1,000, 'What's the name of Posh Spice's famous footballing husband?' and you blurt out 'David Blunkett'. I just seemed to go a bit blank at the easiest of tasks. Breathing steadily appears to make it easier, but when I took the mouthpiece out, that was just the problem – temporarily I couldn't breathe, which is freaky.

Like so many things in life however, practice makes perfect: what starts out being scary soon becomes fine once you've done it a few, oh, alright then, five, six, maybe it was 10 (I lost count) times.

Although I eventually mastered this in-and-out business, dimbo that I was, I couldn't see the point in deliberately taking away your one source of air while underwater. Why, in Heaven's name, would any person with a vested interest in their own survival do this? There is method however in the madness. As my instructor patiently explained, your regulator may get knocked out by another diver kicking you accidentally, for instance, and you would need to know how to get it back in, purge the water and begin breathing again without flying into a mad panic. Good point.

A right eyeful

With the breathing and the replacing of the regulator over and done with, I definitely felt it was time to have a break. Not so. They don't let you off that easily. There is another thing to master before completing your first session and this is much worse than the removal of the mouthpiece, especially if you wear contact lenses. They make you half fill your own mask with water. Yuck. The sensation is alarming. In comes the water and bang goes your vision. First reaction? Panic of course, even though you've been told that to get the water out again is actually quite easy. Easy eh? So what you do is this: you hold your mask against your forehead and prise it off the lower part of your face. By looking up while blowing out through your nose, a little bit like magic, the water does actually disappear from your mask! It's so amazing, that it is actually quite good fun to try it over and over again. I've still not worked out quite how it works, but it does, so what the matter. That's how to clear your mask of water if it begins to trickle in.

Fine, let's go! Breathing underwater, regulator in and out, and how to clear your mask of water. It should definitely be teatime by now ... but, eh, no. 'What happens if your mask gets completely knocked off while diving?' asked my instructor. 'Well, I'd be completely up the Swanee' is what I wanted to say. I wear contact lenses so I'd have to close my eyes, then I wouldn't be able to see a thing – not very good if out in the ocean, really. It didn't seem like the correct answer, so I listened out for the next set of instructions. What I needed to know was how to put a mask back on that would be completely full of water. Oh the thought of it! Claustro— No! No! Change your point of view, this is possible. Others have done it: you can too. Other people wear contact lenses; this is not the end of the world. You are in a swimming pool. You are safe. And so it was back to being underwater. Off came the mask. Eyes tightly clenched. Put it back on, press the top bit on your forehead ... and exhale. Oh, it worked. There was a bit of water left in, so I repeated the process and ... bingo! The mask was no longer an aquarium, I could see, and that was Mission Accomplished. Yippee! We all got a little pat on the back after that exercise.

Under pressure

The great thing about the pool session is that you build gently, gently, one skill on top of the other, which is just as well since there was more to learn. Two more to be precise. The next task was to do a bit of swimming around, slightly deeper than in the very shallow water in which we had completed the first exercises. Not to gawp at the legs of holidaymakers having a splash about, but to experience what happens to your ears when you go deeper down with your scuba gear on. Physics and I never really got on at school. In fact it was a total mystery to me. Say the very word and I stare vacantly into space. There is no way I'm going into detail here; there are plenty of people and books that can do it better than me. But, in practice, this is what happens. As you go deeper, your ears become a bit uncomfortable because the pressure of the water around you squeezes the air in the spaces in your ears. To bring the pressure in your ears back to normal, you have to pinch your nose and blow against it with your mouth closed. I suddenly realised that this is what you do naturally when the pressure is changing as your plane comes in to land – you are equalising the pressure in your ears. With diving, every metre underwater you go, you need to do the nose-pinching thing to get the pressure back to normal, although in fact as you go deeper you have to do it a bit less often.

Practising was alright and it became obvious pretty quickly that there would be absolutely no way you could dive if you had a head cold and were a bit blocked up, which explained why a poor diver had been turned away from the diving centre that morning for sneezing and having an obvious snuffle. I couldn't believe it at the time. Poor thing. He'd come on holiday specifically to dive, had picked up a bug on the plane and ... poof! Up went his plans in one 'Atishoo!' It didn't seem fair, but Safety First is the golden rule of any well-run diving set-up. There is no way they want a casualty on their books and, if you've any sense, you won't want to be one. This explained why the guy with the cold took the setback with such equanimity. Another lesson learnt – and that one wasn't even part of the course.

All-important air

And so, the last item of the morning's session: learning what to do if your own air supply runs out. Oh my goodness! The moment, the very moment, you get a tad bit confident, they throw a spanner in the works with the suggestion that your air may run out.

'HOW EXACTLY?! WHY?! WHEN?! DOES THIS HAPPEN?!'

I wanted answers and I wanted them fast. Sometimes it turns out that this is because you may use your air up more quickly than you expected, perhaps if the dive was more energetic than you had bargained for. Or maybe you accidentally, for whatever reason, stayed slightly longer underwater than you had anticipated. Anyway, the point is, this can happen. You can end up out of air, underwater. Not a great situation to be in obviously, and one where you need some serious back-up, and quickly.

This is where the person who are diving with, your 'buddy' as they are called in diving parlance, comes in rather handy. Actually, they become your life-saver. In essence, what you do is let them know that you have run out of air. Because you can't talk underwater, as we've already observed, you have to do a rather dramatic, although highly appropriate in my view, 'slitting your throat'-type action with your hand to let them know the problem. Next you have to share your buddy's air. He or she gives you their spare regulator: you pop it in your mouth, purge the water out, and then breathe once. All the while this is going on, you keep looking at each other and hang on to each other for grim death. This, it became instantly clear, was why we all have an extra regulator dangling from another hose attached to the tank. I had been too busy previously to ask what it was for, what with everything else that had been going on. Once you have the extra regulator in your mouth, the idea is to slowly go up until you are both safely at the surface. Phew! Drama over, and the first session was also over after learning that. You may find that you do some of these exercises one day and other bits the next, but essentially, once you have mastered these exercises, then you are ready for the big blue ocean. Yikes!

Time to reflect

As I padded slowly back to the diving centre, I felt rather odd. So many experiences had been squidged into quite a short period of time, and it felt strange. Before any emotions had too long to flourish, there was the palaver of getting out of the dreaded wetsuit. If putting them on is tricky, taking them off is equally so. Having finally liberated myself and helped others do likewise, I was wondering how I really felt about scuba-diving now. I went for a walk to have a think and came across one of my fellow first-timers who was clearly pondering too. 'You looked comfy with all of that,' I ventured.

'It's the third time I've had a go at the pool session,' he replied.

I wasn't sure what to say and suddenly I felt rather clever.

'Each year I try another one of the exercises. Next year I reckon I'm going to make it to the sea.'

Feeling extra-smart by this stage, I was about to say something soothing like 'Oh, well, maybe you're already OK to give it a go,' when he piped up, 'My friend had a diving accident. Wasn't his fault but it happens.' I did not feel like asking what had happened. Then he followed up with, 'Also, I'm terrified of being lost at sea after a dive. Have you seen that film *Open Water*?'

Oh blimey. Lost at sea? Here was a neurosis I hadn't yet considered. I made a mental note not to ever catch that particular movie. *Jaws* had done quite enough damage, I didn't need any more Hollywood scenes filling my already overcrowded head with potential problems I could encounter when out at sea.

I couldn't, however, resist asking a few others back at the hotel if they had seen it. Yep, it seemed that everyone had. Unfortunately it was based on a true story. A couple had been diving and somehow the dive boat had not realised that they were two people short before zooming back to shore. They were never seen again and sharks featured heavily in the movie I'm told.

I remembered the disclaimer form I had to sign before doing my pool course that morning. It read 'Diving is an exciting and demanding activity. When performed correctly, applying correct techniques, it is relatively safe.' The word 'relatively' had never seemed so relevant.

Getting clever with yourself is not a good idea.

Remembering that this is a sport that must be taken seriously at all times is a top priority. It was becoming crystal clear that this wasn't a sport to get all puffed up and over-confident about. Snorkelling is one thing. As long as you are in safe waters, you don't need any complex heavy gear and you can afford to switch off a bit. With scuba-diving, you need your wits about you all the time.

CHAPTER 3

Going down

Of course, the next step is to transfer the basics learnt about scuba-diving in the safety of the pool to the big, open and, in my case, rather dreaded briny. Admittedly we are talking about the Indian Ocean which is a lot warmer than the English Channel off Bognor or Littlehampton, even though I grew up on, and love, the south coast of England. A better temperature the Indian Ocean may be, but it was still a big, vast expanse of, probably shark-infested, water.

I don't know about you, but when I'm nervous, I usually talk too much. I remember when Bob Geldof plonked himself opposite me in my local café on the King's Road. It was his local too, I believe, so he had every right to be there, and there was nowhere else to sit.

After a totally silent breakfast, he mentioned, while getting ready to leave, that he 'liked my top'. Instead of being cool and just saying 'thanks', I blurted out, 'It's from a line in Marks and Spencer's called Per Una which is really good value, has some pretty awful stuff but sometimes does some, well, does some OK stuff too, but then, I'm not sure this would really suit you—' Poor man. He looked totally baffled and virtually sprinted for the door.

That's me when I'm nervous. I babble incoherently. When I'm really, really nervous, however, I go completely silent. And it was in total silence that I sat as the dive boat chugged off and we left the shore behind, heading for my first 'proper' dive. Logic was screaming at me to feign sea sickness and to get Soonan the skipper to turn the boat around and deliver me safely back to the shore. My total lack of speech made that impossible. How I longed to be one of those elegant cross spouses, impatiently rapping a set of beautifully manicured nails on the sun lounger, waiting for her diving other half to return from his seafaring outing.

Bridget-on-sea

And talking of the others, how come *they* all looked so cool and calm? And how dare they be having fun and chatting and laughing when I was a ball of terror? Nothing makes you feel more of an outsider than being smack in the middle of a group of people completely at ease with the task ahead while you are having kittens. This was, no doubt, how my friend Catherine had felt when we took her skiing for her first time. The rest of the group were old timers on the slopes. On her first morning, she did her real-life Bridget Jones imitation on the chairlift, failing to get off, sailing round the end of cable and back down, quite alone, to where we had all first hopped aboard. What goes around comes around. Literally. Here was my penance. In spadefuls. Catherine, I thought, I'm sorry I ended up flat on my back in total hysterics with my skis in the air. I should have raced down to find you, and if you could see me now, you would know that I'm truly, truly …

Clunk. Oh blimey, back to the real world. That was the anchor going over. The engine stopped and, oh gawd, this was the dive site.

The other divers were getting their kit ready by cleaning their masks. Or were they? They seemed to be spitting in them. Yuck. I must ask about that later, I thought, as my mask was passed to me. Flippers (oops, fins) on first. Next, the jacket and tank thing, which, I've forgotten to mention, is called a BCD. (Here we go again, more technical terms!) BCD stands for 'buoyancy control device', which is a bit of a mouthful but essentially means that it's a bit like a balloon: you can pump air into it, which makes you float at the surface (a bit like wearing a lifejacket), or let the air out, which means that you can descend into the water. The same principles apply underwater. Inflating it makes you go up a bit; deflating it makes you go down a bit.

In we go

Anyway, BCD on and clipped up; fins on; mask on; regulator stuffed in my mouth. It was time to sit on the edge of the boat to … oh heavens! Splash! went the first diver off the side of the boat. Splash! went the second. Lawks, was I really going to have to do that too? Fall backwards into the water? Gérald had to be joking. Surely first-timers just get lowered in some other way? Surely … ? I mean, where was the winch? The steps? A little inflatable slide maybe, like you see on the laminated safety-instruction sheets that you get with the in-flight magazines on aeroplanes? Nope, it seemed not. It became obvious that the back-roll was the only way I was going in.

Now this caused our first little hiccup. Yes, I could see the others were fine. No, they hadn't appeared to knock themselves out by bashing their heads on the boat during their semi backwards somersault and obviously, the theory went, I too would be fine. But that's the point, isn't it? The theory is quite, quite different to the practice. To actually

launch yourself instinctively the wrong way off a perfectly seaworthy boat into the sea, weighed down with what felt like 100 tonnes of the most uncomfortable clobber I'd ever come across just didn't compute. I remained firmly pinned to the edge of the boat while my lovely, kind, ultra-patient instructor offered gentle words of encouragement like 'It will be fine, it's not a problem,' and so on and so on.

I was still teetering on the edge, the other divers long gone, when Soonan looked over at me pointedly. Normally, when the divers were all underwater, he was left in peace to bob quietly around in the ocean in charge of the vessel. He looked like he wanted his normal 'me time'. As I was staring at him, disregarding his 'go on' looks, I began fiddling with the clasp of my BCD, beginning to de-kit myself and mumbling down to Gérald something like 'Honestly it's OK, I'll just have a quick sunbathe while you check out the others.'

Suddenly, I felt like I was in real-life version of a Nike ad.

'Just do it. You can,' said Gérald gently. 'Just do it.'

A bit like London cabbies, scuba instructors have been trained to be calm, even when faced with a client who has been procrastinating for a good 20 minutes while he or she patiently bobs around in the waters below, in slightly choppy conditions getting nippier by the moment. I could have forgiven him an outburst but the calmness had far more effect.

In fact, the effect was surprisingly instantaneous. There I was, tumbling backwards with a socking great tank on my back, a massive bit of rubber stuffed in my mouth and a mask clamped on my face trapping within its frames a set of terrified eyes with nostrils flaring like a Grand National winner. And of course the pair of Coco the Clown-proportioned fins on my feet.

Pantomime panicking

It takes about a nanosecond to hit the water and another five being swirled around like you are on a fast spin cycle before you realise that you are still alive. That said, as I popped to the surface, my first reaction was to wrench the regulator from my mouth and to gulp down gallons of real air. The 'back-roll' as it's known in scuba circles was, as it turned out, the easy bit. It's the going down that gets really tough. It was when Gérald popped the dreaded regulator back in my mouth that the real, real panic began to rise. He honestly, honestly had to be kidding. I yanked it out again like some mad scene in a pantomime. 'I just can't,' I panted.

'You can.'

'I can't.'

Now I was beginning to sound like Orville the Duck.

'Look at my eyes. You can. We will go down together.'

If it hadn't been for the look in his eyes saying 'I know you can do this,' I'd probably still be there at the surface. Like any scuba-diving instructor though, Gérald really did know what he was doing, and it is more than any instructor's job and reputation are worth to transfer a beginner from their basic training to an open-water dive without an implicit belief that they can cope with the underwater challenges ahead. This comes back to what Alexander the psychologist was saying. There is a difference between facing and overcoming your fears and knowing when you honestly, honestly shouldn't be giving it a go. You really do have to make this call for yourself, but having an excellent and experienced instructor can help you realise which side of the fence you are actually on.

For me it seemed that I could, and so it was time to let the air out of the BCD and actually begin descending. Little by little down we went. I'd like to say that it got easier but it didn't. My heart was seriously racing. The choppiness of the water was pulling us around a bit and in spite of clenching his hand as though my life depended on the human contact (actually I think it did, even now when I look back), I was still gulping air down at a very fast rate.

It's amazing how much you can communicate underwater without being able to verbalise things. 'Look at my eyes,' directed Gérald. 'Calm your breathing, in and out, slowly, slowly,' went the signals.

And remarkably, very, very gradually, my breathing did begin to slow down a little, my vice-like grip on his hand, which must by then have been totally lacking circulation, began to ease, and I tentatively looked around a little. Looking up isn't necessarily a good idea I decided early on. I really didn't want to see how far above me the surface was, so I kept looking down instead and then, way-hey! there was a fish. A beautiful, beautiful yellow, white and black striped butterfly fish (not that I knew that was its name at that precise moment in time). Anyway, it was no less beautiful for being nameless, and it swam right past me, totally unperturbed by my presence and absolutely glorious to behold.

Wow! Gérald's photographs had not disappointed. As we gradually made it further down and came upon the coral reef, it was absolutely impossible to feel anything other than sheer, jaw-dropping (although obviously you can't do this if you want to keep the air supply going) awe at the sights all around.

Good Lord. Yes, Good Lord. I'm not especially religious, but from that moment on I have found it hard not to believe that somewhere there is a master creator. How else could all the incredible colours of the fish, the extraordinary shapes of the corals and the wonderful textures of the rocks have been formed? Someone had to have had a hand in all of this I thought as I stared in utter reverence at all before me. And talking of having a hand … gosh! I suddenly looked down and realised that I was no longer holding Gérald's.

Eye-stretching wonder

Obviously he'd witnessed all this a hundred times before. A 'first-timer' going from utter terror to sheer, eye-stretching wonder at the underwater world. As we went slightly, slightly deeper, automatically equalising my ears by pinching my nose as we went (it's amazing how natural this process becomes), the more incredible it all felt.

It was here, gliding around, properly underwater that I realised again how the equipment, so alien and ungainly on dry land, is carried effortlessly in the ocean. And it was as I was meandering peacefully through this extraordinary sub-aquatic environment that I was struck, for real, by the noise. Or rather, the lack of it.

Just like on Gérald's computer movies, there were no sounds of mobiles ringing or bleeping about incoming texts. No cars or plane engines roaring. No peeping of horns, no shouting, no voices. Since almost everything underwater is communicated through sign language, there was just the gentle, regular, rhythmic sound of my own breathing and the bubbles this produced as I finned peacefully, suspended in the water. The slow, deep breaths of diving are often compared to yoga. No wonder the yogis get addicted, I was thinking, then before I knew it Gérald was signalling that it was time to go up.

'Up? Surely not!' I was pleading with my eyes.

Talk about women being fickle. Suddenly the oh-so-reluctant diver didn't want to leave that world filled with wonder, didn't want to be lifted from the soft blue, gentle-on-the-eyes light, didn't want to leave the grey rays sweeping by, their 'wings' carrying them so effortlessly on their way, the octopuses as they pulsated in their hide-outs or the majestic orange and white striped lion fish pottering about their business.

'Up' came the look (and the thumb movement) in response. I knew, but had forgotten in the excitement, that this was totally non-negotiable. If buying a property is about Location, Location, Location, diving is about Planning, Planning, Planning and Safety, Safety, Safety. We had reached our pre-planned safety limit for the time spent at that depth. No questions asked. We were going up. And so we gradually, gradually, eased ourselves away from the gorgeous sights and began our ascent.

Now daring, for the first time, to look up at the surface, I could see the most amazing sight of the sun streaming through the water, light breaking everywhere with an iridescent beauty. I felt as though someone was drenching my whole body with sunbeams. The shafts of light, the streams of bubbles, the sound of our breathing, it was almost overwhelming.

When we finally popped up on the surface, I was beaming. Gérald was beaming. 'So how was your first dive?' I couldn't stop smiling for long enough to answer. Soonan chugged into sight, coming to collect us. Off came the BCD, off came the fins. After Soonan had yanked those into the boat we climbed up the ladder and joined the other divers who were busy chatting about their day's experiences.

Once again I was silent, not in panic this time but in sensory overload. There was simply so much that had taken place in the past hour that it was really hard to take it all in. And so I sat there in total quietness but, this time, feeling peaceful, hearing with delight the others chat excitedly about their sightings and discoveries. As I listened, I began to realise that however many dives you've been on, it appears that you remain stunned, elated, humbled or just delighted by what you see. The sights and feelings of scuba-diving, it seems, continue to thrill long after your first attempts.

Back on dry land

Back at base, gear washed, wetsuits hung up to dry, feet well under the table of the beach-side bar, I found myself stirring a cappuccino and thinking of my conversation with Roz over a similar cup not so very long ago in the King's Road café. How on earth was I going to explain this one?! I could go for the nonchalant option and just text her casually along the lines of: 'U know I said I wldn't dive. Well, gve it a go. It's gr8'. Or maybe I'd tell the truth. 'Words v tasty. Just eaten loads of them. Been diving. Absolutely flipping, life-changingly brilliant'.

I wanted to know more from Gérald. Was I on my first step to becoming a diving bore? 'Oh, definitely, you're on the first rung,' came the reply. 'One day I'm going to take you to one of our dive sites called the Cathedral. It's a large cave with light pouring in from its open end. It has the most incredibly special atmosphere and you think, "Wow am I really seeing this?!" You want to fall to your knees and pray, to say thank you for being alive. People come to dive in Mauritius from all over the world to get even 40 minutes of such precious peace and a time out from their schedules in such a lovely dive site. Seeing the transformation a dive can make to a person is one of the job's biggest pleasures.'

Gosh, the Cathedral sounded like a dive especially worth doing, and I was already daydreaming about it when he brought me up short: 'But first you have to do your courses. To come with me to the Cathedral you have to be an advanced diver. So it's off to the classroom for you – you'll have to do your Open Water Course first.'

Back to school

Oh no. I was on top of the world; the last thing I wanted to hear was that this fun, this special, special fun, was going to be ruined by going back to the classroom. But he wasn't joking. What I had just done was a 'try-dive'. Scuba-diving is serious stuff, and if you are going to do it, you need to bite the bullet and learn about the sport. You need to relearn your school physics (or, in my case, learn it for the first time) and study books and videos, depending on which course you take. Then you need to carry out all the practical underwater exercises to show you really have mastered your mask-clearing and your alternate air-source buddy breathing and that you understand all of your equipment. On top of all that, horror of horrors, you need to do a written test. I wasn't sure I liked the sound of all this. No, that's not true: I definitely didn't like the sound of all this. I thought I'd left lessons and exams well behind.

I already loved Mauritius and was making regular trips before I thought about diving. As I'm a journalist I can pretty much write from anywhere and so I decided to really get stuck in and start the learning process. I dedicated the mornings and early afternoons to my own work and, in the late afternoons, strolled off to the classroom at the Sun Diver centre. Yet the funny thing was, as soon as the classroom teaching began, I forgot that I was missing my beach time and tried really hard to understand the lessons.

I found myself reading the accompanying books and manuals instead of my usual Jeffrey Archer on the sun-lounger, and I even discovered that there was an incentive to get my poor brain around the physics of it all. It was not, I have to say, easy. In three years of instructing, Gérald admitted, he never come across anyone, from 13-year-olds to 60-year-olds, who was quite so dim when it came to grasping the fundamentals of water density, the effect it has on the volume of air in the body's air spaces or the calculation of dive times using dive tables. On several occasions we, or rather I, had tantrums and tears, but if I was going down in the future, to further depths and to meet new challenges and discover new experiences, somehow this information had to be drummed into my head.

You simply have to know what you are doing when diving, and that means getting on with the theory, however much you'd rather be underwater, pootling around with the fish instead. That said, the training is not all classroom-based. You do get to dive as well and learn how to start putting the theory into practice. It was hard not to muse, after that first try-dive day, how odd it was that I could go from dealing with the absolute nightmare of bobbing around on the surface, deflating the buoyancy jacket while gasping for air and thinking this was the worst and scariest thing I'd ever done in my life to breathing underwater for real and feeling that it was absolutely the best experience of my life. The gamut of emotions, through every moment of that day, remains as vivid now as then, and all I can say is that if I can do it, there are plenty of you out there who can manage it too.

Girl power

Obviously this is a wild generalisation, but it seems to me, after asking around, that it is us girls who tend to be the most hesitant when it comes to the prospect of scuba diving. Which may help explain why women account for only 35 per cent of all recreational divers. Perhaps this is down to our lower levels of the 'he man' hormone, testosterone, which naturally drives men to take risks and have that 'go for it' attitude to life.

Maybe this naturally makes blokes less neurotic. When I was filling in my disclaimer form, every time I saw a box asking 'Do you have X,Y or Z problem?', my immediate reaction was to ask 'Why do you want to know that?' and I couldn't tick the box until I had my answer.

Blokes just seem to tick boxes without even looking up. 'Have I had recurring complicated migraine headaches or do I take medication to prevent them?', 'Nope', 'X'. 'Have I had blackouts or fainting (full/partial loss of consciousness)?', 'Nope', 'X'.

Or maybe it is just because Western women were slower off the starting blocks when it came to scuba diving. After all, in the early 20th century, we were still being carted out to the shallow waters in Brighton in bathing huts, bedecked from top to toe in the most unfetching of bathing bonnets, billowing blouses, long skirts, rubber slippers and, just to be absolutely sure our modesty was preserved, thick dark-coloured 'hose'.

Simone Cousteau, wife of the famous Jacques, took no notice of conventional views of women and water and donned an Aqualung way back in the 1940s. Many more brave female souls have followed in her footsteps since. But statistics still show us girls to be lagging behind when it comes to getting in a wetsuit and going down.

The good news is that we actually have some anatomical advantages over men when it comes to scubering. Because we and our lungs are smaller, we need less oxygen and so may not need such a big tank. However, we do – in spite of our extra fat – get cold more rapidly. This is worth bearing in mind when selecting the thickness of your wet or dry suit. Don't be guided by what the blokes are doing.

Otherwise, all things being equal, there is no reason why we shouldn't enjoy scuba diving as much as our male counterparts.

And oh, one last thing. I heard a girl chirp up when she got to the 'Have you ever had chest surgery?' section: 'Do boob jobs count?' Everyone went completely silent then burst out laughing.

Gérald looked it up in his faithful book *Diving and Subaquatic Medicine* and, according to its eminent authors, implants have been exposed to various conditions of simulated dives and apparently they are pretty safe. However, they don't recommend deep diving followed by flying. Just in case you were wondering. So Pamela Anderson, Jordan: if you are reading this, take it from me, it is safe to dive.

CHAPTER 4

What can go wrong...
but usually doesn't

As I was descending into the depths on later dives (we only went down to about 15 metres, but it felt like the depths), the initial panic of actually being underwater had subsided. However, much to my surprise, all kinds of other potential life-ending problems came racing into my mind that I'd never considered when first starting out. What if my tank exploded? What if the guy at the diving centre hadn't actually put air in my tank? What if my instructor had a seizure? What if the piece of rubber hose carrying air from my tank to my mouth became blocked? What if, what if, what if. There don't seem to be any specific hand signals for 'Oh blimey, my tank has just blown up!'

I'm the kind of person to whom, if things can go wrong, they quite often do. Memories of my dippier 'things going wrong' moments swirled around my brain intermingling with the potential underwater problems. As if from nowhere I began to think of a particularly important lunch meeting I once had with a journalist. I decided that, for once, I would try extra especially hard to look the part. A manicure would be a nice idea, I thought, and so off I went (in plenty of time I might add), to have my nails primped and painted before lunch. I may have been in good time, but the manicurist wasn't and by the time I finished and got out into a searingly hot London day, I was running late. Was there a taxi in sight? Of course not. So for some reason that I've never quite worked out, I began jogging down the road in my high heels and beautiful silk wraparound skirt in search of an elusive black cab – as though running would somehow make one materialise more quickly.

As I jogged I felt a sense that all was not right in the lingerie department. Something concerning my bra had come loose. The problem, it turned out, was that the pretty front lace-uppy ribbon had become completely untied. That was the bad news; the good news was that I could stop jogging, because a cab drew up. In I hopped and began to retie the bow but, blast, the nail varnish wasn't dry. My nails had gone from beautiful to dog's dinner in 30 seconds of furtive under-my-top tussling. 'Stop!' I yelled at the cabbie. 'Sorry, I mean, please would you mind stopping at a pharmacist's?' He did and I rushed in and out again, hopping in armed with a tub of Quickies, little pads pre-soaked in nail-varnish remover.

On arrival at the restaurant I rushed directly to the ladies cloakroom to rectify the mess. As luck wouldn't have it, the venue was a new restaurant with a temporary cloakroom the size of a telephone box. The toilet and the sink were, as Miss Henson my geography teacher would say when describing housing in Brazilian ghettos, 'cheek by jowl'. Not much room for manoeuvring, in other words and, as it happened, not a bin in sight. After cleaning my nails, I popped the Quickies into the toilet, pulled the chain and began to turn towards the door, only to find myself being pulled backwards. Heaven to Betsy … my flowing silk skirt was disappearing down the loo. Having won a closely run fight for ownership of the skirt, I tentatively ventured back

upstairs, it dripping wet and flapping around my legs.
I didn't look sophisticated. I looked an utter mess and, as
the waiter asked with a wry grin, 'Is this the new wet look,
Madam?', I felt an utter prawn. But I had lunch with the
journalist – soaking wet, nail-varnish free and with wonky
lingerie to boot.

Some important questions

Since no one who knows me is in the least bit surprised by
these regular occurrences, when I voiced my concerns on the
phone to my best friend Jane regarding things such as self-
combusting tanks, she took me surprisingly seriously. 'Well,
you'd better ask. I mean, if it's going to happen to anyone, it's
going to be you.' I took my instructor aside after one of my
training dives and grasped the nettle, 'Gérald, um, what do
you think the chances are of my tank exploding underwater?
I mean, you know, it's got all that compressed air in it. What
happens if it's too big a strain and it goes bang?'

'What?'

'What happens if … '

'I heard what you said, it's just that – no, of course it's not
going to explode.'

'Well, has one ever exploded?'

'Yes, I've heard of one exploding when it was being filled
with air in the compressor room.'

'In that case, why couldn't it happen underwater?'

'It could.'

'Well, then what if it does?'

'It won't.'

'Why not?'

'Because we service our tanks and it just won't. And I've

never, ever heard of anyone to whom it has happened in practice, and there are a lot of diving centres in Mauritius.'

And that was that. Not satisfied, I emailed the people who monitor diving accidents worldwide (the Divers Alert Network). I have to confess, there were some strokes and heart attacks happening underwater but no obvious 'tank blew up' category that I could find. Right, cross that one of the list then. 'Tank explosions: very, very unlikely.'

Instructor having a coronary artery: possible.

'Gérald.'

'Yes? What now?'

'Do you eat a lot of butter?'

Oh alright then, I didn't really ask him that, but I did feel like it. Although maybe I should have been getting my own cholesterol levels double-checked. It seems to me that sometimes recreational divers don't appear to give much consideration to their own physical fitness and yet diving is such an incredibly stressful sport to the body. It's all very well checking that your equipment is in good working order, that your tank is full (well-serviced and crack and rust free), but what about your own blood vessels? Are they free from fatty build-ups that could trigger a heart attack? Is your blood pressure high? This could lead to a stroke. Believe me, if these things happen underwater, you don't have much of a chance of survival, buddy or no buddy.

That said, a very heroic dive master friend called Brain did actually manage to save the life of a middle-aged gentleman who was diving with him. The man had a mild heart attack at about 15 metres and lost consciousness underwater. Brian not only managed to get the unconscious man to the surface, still breathing, by using special 'rescue' skills, but also gave him mouth to mouth resuscitation while they were bobbing around on the waves, before dragging him into the boat.

It is to avoid such potential problems occurring underwater that everyone should have a full medical before beginning their diving courses. And if you have any sense, regardless of the specific requirements of the particular dive body you are affiliated to, you should have one regularly thereafter. It is hard to stress the importance of this and even if you come across centres that don't seem to insist on it, do it for your own sake. It's your life.

The same goes for just general well-being. It's absolutely crazy to dive when tired or hung-over or even when feeling a bit under the weather. If you are not on the ball you can make small mistakes that can put you and your buddy in danger. It's just not worth the risk.

Taking responsibility for yourself includes making sure you only do dives that you know you are up to: physically, psychologically and technically. If after getting to the dive site you discover that the visibility is poorer than you thought, if the water is colder, if there is more current than you expected, then just remember there are two words that you *are* allowed to use. Learning to say 'No thanks, this dive is not for me' can stop things from going wrong that really don't need to.

A friend called Dylan, a regular at Sun Divers, says that he sometimes feels that 'the sea just doesn't want him'. If you get this feeling, then it's better to just trust it rather than go against it and dive. If it means letting down your buddy at the surface, this is better than letting them down underwater, when you may put both their safety and yours in peril.

Booze and ciggies

It goes without saying that alcohol before a dive is seriously out of the question. The last thing you need is any impairment of judgement and if alcohol doesn't do that effectively enough on terra firma, when your body is at depth and under pressure, the mind-altering effects are even more profound. Nor is it a good idea to tuck into booze straight after a dive. Doing so can make you more prone to decompression sickness, a nasty problem that arises when your body cannot deal with getting rid of all the nitrogen that you absorb from the air that you breath while diving.

And smoking? Well, I probably hardly need to address that one. The best advice you can give a smoking diver is to give up. The next best advice is to avoid having a ciggie for a couple of hours before going down. You don't need to be a doctor to work out that the smoke and chemicals surging around your lungs and blood vessels interfere with your circulation and breathing. Smoking increases the risk of heart disease and strokes for everyone, and for divers it can up your chances of air getting trapped in your lungs, which could then over-expand and become very seriously damaged. It can be curtains if that happens.

A criminal error

All these rather serious issues aside, there are the small practical details that you have to watch out for as well, as I've discovered to my cost. It is a big fault of mine that I run around in such haste in my everyday life and often don't pay attention to practical detail. One morning I was darting off to a meeting in London, this time a breakfast at the Savoy

Hotel with the author of the sun-lounging novels, Mr [this was before his Lord days] Jeffrey Archer. The idea was for me to interview him about his favourite breakfast. (As a nutritionist who writes, I get the odd assignment like this – sadly not yet with Brad Pitt, but I'm waiting.)

Anyway, on the way, I suddenly decided that I didn't like my outfit and darted into the only clothing shop open at 8am, a Benetton store in Victoria train station. There was a blue suit hanging up, right size, right shape, yep, it fitted. 'Fine, I'll have it and wear it if that's OK with you,' I said to the assistant while grappling for my credit card. 'No problem, here are your other clothes Madam,' she said handing me a bag. Off I jogged for a cab. To cut a long story short, I got to the Savoy, sat down for breakfast with Jeffrey Archer, gabbled away (I was nervous) and took my jacket off. Quite normal behaviour I thought, yet his eyes seemed transfixed. Glancing down I could see why. The big white security tag was proudly on display. 'I didn't … if that's what you're thinking,' I garbled, '… nick this, actually. It's just that I didn't like what I was wearing this morning and … Oh God. Look, the security-alarm system can't have been on in Benetton. Oh, yes, scrambled eggs please. So, what's your favourite breakfast, Mr Archer?'

Little details

But I've had to break this habit when it comes to diving. Not paying attention to the small details just doesn't pay when others' safety and yours is at stake. Really simple things can lead to much bigger problems. Like, for instance, just taking the wrong size wetsuit. If you squeeze yourself into one which is too tight – maybe it's your own, you've put on a few pounds and don't want to admit it to yourself and buy a new one, or maybe you are being polite and not making a fuss when the dive centre hands you one which is OK, but a bit on the small size – then think again. Change it for one that does fit, because when they are too small they can trigger claustrophobia and stress and, if tight around the neck, can squeeze your carotid artery and reduce blood flow to your brain. Not a good idea.

Equally, if your fins don't fit properly and are a tad too big, then they can fall off during the dive, stopping you from being able to fin through the water properly and causing you to lose propulsion and get worn out and stressed from flapping your legs too much. While most of us don't have all our own kit and rely on our dive centre to provide us with tanks and regulators that are in tiptop condition, it is down to us as individuals to check these simple things.

Whether your tank has air in it is, for instance, rather a major thing not to check. I sidled up to Ken, a lovely dive master at Sun Divers who was filling some tanks and mused, 'Ken, how likely do you suppose it would be that you'd miss a tank?'

'Impossible,' he replied without hesitation. 'Not here. But it can happen. If you don't go to a good dive centre and you don't check your tank is full before diving then, sure, it can.'

Crikey. Lesson Number goodness-knows-what. Check your tank before setting off. No air or a half-filled tank could be rather more of a problem than forgetting to have your security tag taken off in Benetton. 'How about the hose thingy from the tank to the regulator Ken? Could that get, well, blocked or something?'

What can go wrong ... but usually doesn't **55**

'Very rarely gets blocked,' said Ken.

'But it can explode,' said Gérald, who was passing. Yikes, back to exploding things. 'The good news,' Gérald continued, 'is that should this happen, your air does not cut out immediately and although you can hear the explosion going off with a bang behind you and can see bubbles come zooming out from behind you, air doesn't come crashing into your mouth, whizzing down to over-inflate your lungs.'

'Well, that's a relief,' I thought. You do, however, need to get to your buddy's alternative air supply pretty rapidly so that you can resume breathing. Once again, checking your hose is in good condition with a visual once-over should stop this ever happening to you. There is really no point in leaving this kind of thing to chance. If you go to a reputable diving centre, there is little chance a blockage will happen, but taking responsibility for your own gear is the name of the game.

Check and double-check

Checking that you have a sound hose set and enough air in your tank before you set off on your dive is only a fraction of the story. It helps just a tad if your air supply is turned on before you back-roll, as I once discovered when 5 metres down, holding onto the anchor line, waiting for others to follow from the boat. As I inhaled, my breaths seemed to be getting harder and harder to take. Eventually I realised, to my horror, that my air was just not coming through at all. Eeeek! I was hoping to never have to use that drastic 'out of air' signal, the one with the slitting action across my throat. But suddenly I was at it with ever more desperate sawing motions. Thank heavens Gérald was just behind and realised immediately what was going on. He stuffed his spare regulator in my mouth and immediately checked the status of the valve on the back of my tank. 'It helps if you turn your air supply on.' He couldn't actually say this of course, but it was written all over his face. Did I feel daft? Yes. Do I check and double-check that my own and my buddy's air supplies are on every single time? Absolutely. Without fail. You only make that mistake once.

I soon discovered that the things that stop you diving tend to be down to your own errors rather than exploding tanks and tubing. Take forgetting an essential piece of gear, for example. Like your fins. I'd gaily boarded the boat one morning full of the pre-dive joys of life, chit-chatted away to fellow divers, admired the view, spat in my mask (honestly, this is what you do to clean it: spit, rub around then rinse with seawater – it's a bit gruesome, but it does the trick), checked my BCD, and so on. Then just as we dropped the anchor, I reached for my fins. Which fins? The fins that were back in the dive centre. No fins, no diving. Once again, did I feel stupid? Yep. Once again, I haven't repeated the mistake.

Warding off illness

There are other things that can stop you from diving, such as your physical make-up, which could be put down to the luck of the draw. Like seasickness. Thankfully it's not something I've ever been especially prone to. Sailing a treacherous sea from Southampton to Bilbao in Spain when I was little, my mum and I were virtually the only passengers onboard to make it to the breakfast table. I remember the huge fun we had grabbing our porridge bowls as they sped across the table if we let go of the side of them. We spent an enjoyable passage up on deck while the others were groaning in their cabins below.

Seasickness is a bit of a dive-stopper. If you're susceptible, my best advice is to carry something with ginger in it on every dive. It is not just an old wives' tale that ginger helps to quell nausea. Super-nutrients in ginger have been shown to boost our production of digestive fluids, which helps to neutralise the acids in the stomach that trigger motion sickness. In fact, naval cadets taking 1 gram of powdered ginger a day were found, in one piece of research, to be far less likely to suffer from cold sweats and vomiting, both classic symptoms of seasickness, than those who took a dummy powder. Although powdered ginger has been used in trials, it is not very convenient or palatable compared to a chunk of fresh ginger that you can chew on. If you do not fancy this idea, then try drinking some flat ginger ale (fizzy is not a good idea before diving because it fizzes in your intestines and makes you burp), or eating some ginger biscuits, both of which can be really calming and helpful. Ginger is most effective when taken several hours before your boat journey as well as during the trip.

Prevention is better than cure

The dreaded head cold is another of those annoying 'things that can go wrong' and can stop your diving plans in their tracks. Begin the preventive action a good 30 days before you set off for a diving trip. (Actually, this is good advice all year round to help avoid colds.) Start by taking a supplement every day of multivitamins and minerals that contain 100 per cent of the daily recommended intake, preferably one that also contains a probiotic mix of bacteria as well. Multibionta is a great example and has been proven to both reduce the number of colds that people catch as well the severity of the symptoms and the duration by a good two days. On a precious diving holiday, every day counts. If you cannot get hold of any Multibionta, then it is well worth taking a standard multivitamin and mineral supplement and also one of those little yoghurty-style drinks that contain probiotics.

In addition, I would advise herbal extracts to further help to boost your immune system. It is well worth contacting The Organic Pharmacy in London (www.theorganicpharmacy.com) and ordering two things on-line. First, a bottle of their Immune Tonic and, second, a bottle of their Immune Tincture. Ten days before setting off on your diving holiday, take the Immune Tonic. You just drop some into a glass each day and drink it down. If you feel any slight infection coming on, replace this with the Immune Tincture. While the former helps to shore up your immune system and to help prevent catching a cold virus, the latter helps to knock bugs on the head if you have picked any up. At the same time, if you feel a snuffle coming on, wolf down up to 1000 milligrammes of Vitamin C daily until it is has completely gone. Take all of these with you on your break away. They are the best way to keep colds at bay and to minimise the symptoms and the time you are lumbered with them.

If ear infections are a problem for you, then I suggest that you start chewing gum – specifically sugar-free gum like Orbit, which is sweetened with the natural sugar alternative called xylitol. Xylitol comes from a birch tree in Finland and has the most wonderful 'anti-stick' properties. It moves from your mouth as you chew and up into the tube that runs between your mouth and your ear. Once in this tube, xylitol quite literally acts as non-stick coating, helping to stop the bacteria that cause middle-ear infections from taking hold. Chewing gum with xylitol, sucking mints like Smints, or using a new granulated form that you can stir into teas and coffees like sugar (called XyloBrit) are some ways of helping to both prevent pre-diving ear infections and protect you from picking them up in swimming pools when you do arrive at your diving destination.

Looking after yourself

Going to a reputable diving centre with well-maintained equipment, checking and double-checking your buddy's gear and your own, making sure your tank is full and the air is on and remembering to take all the essentials for diving with you will help to stop things going wrong underwater. Taking care of your health will help prevent problems occurring and helps you get more out of your diving. The more on top of things you are, the less likely you are to stress and the more likely you are to have a happy, fun and safe time underwater. I've accepted that I can't ever stop a shark appearing from nowhere, but I am now pretty certain that my tank isn't going to go bang, so that's one more neurosis I've crossed off the list. As for the other potential problems, averting them, it seems, is largely down to me.

That's not to say that on the odd morning I won't trudge off to the boat with the lovely Bibi, the receptionist at Sun Divers, running after me swirling my mask above her head, but I do double-check when I'm on the boat, because there's just no room for being dippy when diving.

CHAPTER 5

A challenging student

I didn't exactly excel at maths at school. When Mrs Dubben my maths teacher used to peer down over me and my textbook and demand to know how long it would take a train travelling at 60 miles per hour to reach the person at the station that was 5 miles away, she may as well have been asking in Swahili. I would be imagining myself tied to the track like one of those crinolined damsels in distress in a black and white western, seeing in my mind's eye the train coming at me full tilt. If I didn't answer the question in one minute, I would be run over. Quick, quick, what's the answer?! Yet even the imagined imminent threat of being squelched on the track didn't help. I couldn't tell Mrs Dubben what she wanted to hear, because things like that simply make no sense to me. I am not, as my 'extra' maths teacher Mr Lawry sighed, when attempting to drag me through my O-Level, 'a numbers person'.

Physics was just as impossible. If an elephant weighed 2 tons standing on its four feet, exerting a pressure of heaven-knows-what spread between them, try as I might, I had absolutely no idea how much pressure there would be were it to stand on one. Or, for that matter, when the tirelessly patient Professor Danielle tried to put it into terms he felt a blonde might understand, were it standing in two pairs of Marilyn Monroe's stilettos? I hadn't a clue, as I struggled with this and many more unfathomable problems in the somewhat embarrassingly named 'Remedial Physics' class

I'd been thrown into at university to sort out my obvious lack of aptitude in the subject. Since I was studying nutrition and was clearly erring towards the less hard-nosed laboratory-based end of Physics, I think that he forgave me, and I sat patiently and quietly while the others got to grips with the laws of thermodynamics.

I knew enough to understand that as Walter de la Mare wrote in his poem 'Miss T', 'It's a very odd thing/As odd as can be/That whatever Miss T. eats/Turns into Miss T.' It was all I needed to know really, a poet's interpretation of Hippocrates' words 'You are what you eat'. And if you eat too much, you will gain weight. And so I sat there, staring out of the window at the lovely architecture of the church spire on London's Strand, while the inner workings of the universe flew over my head, up up and away, joining the birds as they soared over the pretty weather vane.

Practical applications

Maybe I should have concentrated harder because, like most things in life, the laws of physics have a habit of coming round and nipping you on the bum just when you are least expecting them to – like when you are trying to learn the theory of diving. As I mentioned before, it was a rude awakening to discover that I could not just pootle around in the water with a tank on my back, eyes agog at the marine life, but that I was required to learn about how scuba-diving worked. As the words 'volume' and 'pressure' began to crop up I suddenly felt myself regress immediately into the classes of Mrs Dubben and poor, patient Professor Danielle and, with that, my mind, as then, shut firmly down.

The reason you need to know this theoretical stuff is straightforward enough. Diving is not natural, and in order to do it we have to put our bodies under all sorts of weird stresses and strains. Understanding how your body interacts with the underwater environment allows you to dive safely. It can save your life and the lives of others. It can stop you making mistakes such as going down too deep for too long or extending your dive for longer than planned. Knowing the science can help you to come up safely without blasting your lungs to pieces, and to recognise symptoms in yourself and others if things begin to go wrong during and after a dive. Effectively, you can't dive safely without knowing this stuff. It quickly became apparent that this time I really *was* going to be the crinolined lady mangled on the track if I didn't make a Herculean effort to comprehend what the teachers, books and videos were trying to drum into my resistant skull.

Back to school

I learnt to dive the PADI way. PADI stands for Professional Association of Diving Instructors. There are lots of other schools, for instance CMAS (The Confédération Mondiale des Activités Subaquatiques), set up to provide international standards for divers, or BSAC (British Sub Aqua Club) in the UK. PADI gets you through the basics through a combination of watching videos, reading the manuals and doing lots of little tests and some slightly longer ones. It basically holds your hand, which worked well for me.

The first theoretical lesson described the whole business of whether, quite literally, you sink or swim. If you were wearing a life jacket, you would float. If you didn't and someone tied a whole load of rocks to your feet, you would sink. Once you've understood that, you've got the gist of buoyancy – although there are lots of complicated ways of explaining it in detail. When diving, you will want to be able to sink into the water, because otherwise there would have been no point to struggling into all that gear just to bob around on the surface like a snorkeller. This is where your BCD, the jacket to which your tank is attached, comes in handy. This can have air pumped into it (the air comes from an attachment to your tank) by pressing a 'buoyancy control device' and air removed by pressing another button that allows the air to escape, known as 'the purge'.

To go down, you need to get the air out so that you become less buoyant. Most divers also wear weights, often attached to a belt around the waist, to ensure they are heavier and do go down. Once you are underwater, it is good to remember that breathing out also means you go down a bit, because when you breathe in and your lungs are inflated they are a bit like a balloon that makes you 'lighter'. When they are empty you are less buoyant and go down a bit.

As you go down in the water when you scuba-dive, there is more pressure on your body. Your muscles and your bones are not affected by the pressure as much as the bits of your body that have air spaces, your lungs for instance. If you were to dive down in the water without scuba gear, the deeper you got, the more pressure there would be on your lungs and the more compressed and smaller they would become. When you go from 0 to 10 metres down, the pressure doubles. It doubles again from 10 to 30 metres and again from 30 to 70 metres. Each time, the amount of air your lungs can contain halves. As you go up again, there is less pressure on your body and your lungs expand again.

It is not just your lungs that get squished up as you go down. Other parts of your body that contain air, such as the space in your middle ear, get squeezed too, which takes us right back to one of those first lessons learnt in the pool. This is why you have to pinch your nose regularly on the way down and blow against it. Doing so helps to keep the pressure in the air space equal to that of the water around you and stops your ear drum from imploding under the pressure. A ruptured eardrum is not something you want to experience. Air also gets pressurised in our sinuses, but thankfully they tend to readjust themselves naturally unless you have blocked sinuses which rule out diving completely; it would be too painful.

If you were wearing scuba gear and breathed air in at 10 metres, your lungs would be the same size as at the surface. If you then went up, accidentally holding your breath, that air in your lungs would double in volume and your lungs would expand too much and be seriously damaged. This could even be fatal. You may not think this is very likely to happen, but it can actually happen quite easily if you don't control your buoyancy. If there is too much air in your BCD, you might zip up from 10 metres to the surface, hardly realising that you are zooming up and, in a state of panic, might not remember or have a chance to breath out slowly and surely. Going up slowly and in a controlled way, with steady, regular breaths, helps your lungs to readjust to the reduction in pressure and to remain intact.

Just as when you are at the surface and want to float you add air to your BCD, if you want to rise a little bit when in the water (to get off the bottom for instance), then you squirt in a bit of air and up you go. If you wanted to go down a bit, you would purge air out of your BCD. When you are coming up, you can help to control your speed with your BCD. Letting air out keeps you from going up too fast. Really good divers can also control the speed at which they are going up by controlling and adjusting the volume of air in their lungs … but that's another story.

Nasty nitrogen

Being able to control the speed at which you go up is vital for another reason. When we breathe in air as we go about our normal day-to-day lives up here on the earth's surface, it contains not just oxygen but also other gases such as nitrogen. This nitrogen dissolves in the watery spaces in the body where it does no harm. When you dive, the pressure of the water drives this nitrogen into your muscles, bones and virtually every cell in your body. As you come up, it is vital to do so slowly so that this nitrogen has a chance to come out of these tissues and you are allowed to breathe the excess out through your lungs. If you come up too quickly, this causes nitrogen bubbles to form, which can get trapped everywhere, including your joints and in the blood that's whizzing around your body. This is called decompression sickness. Getting nitrogen stuck in the joints is painful. Getting nitrogen stuck in the blood vessels that supply the lungs, heart and brain can be fatal. I didn't need to know much more than that to understand just how vital it is to get pretty damn au fait with controlling my buoyancy.

Obviously there is a load more to the whole theoretical caboodle than this, and you need to go and learn it properly with qualified instructors. All this little lot took me rather a long time to get my brain round. My instructor Gérald would never have said that I was a little slow in grasping the theory. He said I was virtually in reverse. I eventually got to grips with the whole, tricky business after he resorted to life-size

68 A challenging student

drawings of lungs and stick-men divers. He had the patience of a saint, and I tested him to his limit. I am hugely grateful that he stuck with it. I am absolutely sure that virtually everyone will grasp things more rapidly than I did and will have fewer tears and moments of bewilderment than I. If I had to recall the one main message that came through loud and clear during the first classroom session it was this: 'DON'T HOLD YOUR BREATH AT ANY TIME – KEEP BREATHING.'

The weird thing is that even though I know this in theory, it seems that it is surprisingly easy to forget in practice when you are just starting out, and especially easy the closer you get to the crucial last 10 metres of the dive. I had an overwhelming desire, on my first few dives, to look up and think, 'Great, there's the surface, let's just go up shall we? I've had a lovely time, I'm getting a bit parky, and I'd quite like to hop back in the boat if that's OK.' But it's not OK because, as you have read, the pressure of the water on your body doubles between the surface and 10 metres and so if you zoom up, not going steadily and slowly and breathing regularly but holding your breath and ascending at a rate of knots, your lungs will double their size and potentially go pop.

Added to this is the fact that at 5 metres down you always have to wait for 3 minutes for a 'safety stop'. Different teaching organisations may give slightly varying depths for this, but everyone has to do such a stop. It may seem a bit pointless hanging around when you are so close to getting out, but these 3 minutes give your body extra time to get rid of as much of that excess nitrogen from your tissues as possible. For experienced divers who dive deep, 'decompression stops' (as they are known) take place at various depths on the way up, again to allow nitrogen to be released. If divers go down to 60 metres, for example, they have to have quite a number of decompression stops on the way up to reduce their nitrogen levels.

When you are starting out this is not an issue, because you do not dive deep. However, if you find you have overshot your planned time at a particular depth, then you have to do other stops on the way up as well. Again, how you deal with this depends slightly on the organisation you learn with, but it brings me to the subject of how you work out for how long, at which depths, you can stay underwater. Oh yes, this was fun and games, this bit: the dive tables.

Dive tables

Scientists have worked out, in theory, how long the average human being, male or female, can stay at certain depths and be able to get rid of sufficient nitrogen to avoid problems of decompression sickness. These theoretical calculations can be found in dive tables. They tell you the maximum amount of time you can stay at a certain depth and, if you plan a second dive on the same day, they take your first dive into account to tell you how long you have at a certain depth for the next one. Since the tables are worked out on maximum times at depths for the average man or woman, it's very wise to base your dives on the safest times and not push yourself to the maximum, since who of us can honestly say we are 'average'?

It's hard to explain how to use the tables; you have to get stuck in and get on with it. Fortunately, most people now have diving computers that tell you exactly how long you have been down and will tell you how many stops you need to do if you have exceeded your dive plan. The problem with relying just on a computer is that they may just possibly go wrong, and they don't take into account how much air you have used. By far the best way is to plan your dive with the dive tables and to use a computer as well, and then to keep it in mind all the way through your dive. This way you really understand what you are doing and will probably feel more confident about your dive. You will know in your mind how long you can stay at a certain depth for (this is called 'the bottom time'). Using the dive tables also allows you to build in the potential effects of things that your computer won't know: if you know the water is cold or the conditions a bit tough physically, for instance, then you need to build in extra safety time and be even more conservative than usual.

It's no good just relying on tables and computers though. Most computers won't tell you how much air you have left in your tank. A gauge that you have within easy sight while diving, attached to a hose that is in turn attached to the top of the tank gives you this essential information. You need to check your air regularly: sometimes you can use up air more quickly, and it's no good thinking that a certain amount will automatically last a certain time.

Extra legwork

I was surprised to find my air was running down more rapidly than usual on a recent dive, until I remembered that I was using a different pair of fins. My regular pair are quite long and propel me through the water effortlessly. The small ones

I was wearing on this particular day were nothing like as effective. It took more effort to fin and so, of course, I used up more air.

It is also essential to bear in mind that you use up air faster the deeper you go. Another day I found my air supply to be less than usual when, having back-rolled in, my extra regulator (or 'alternate air supply' in diving lingo) had popped out of the clip designed to keep it in place, and the force of my plopping into the ocean had caused air to rush out. It was a real pain that half of my supply had gone when this happened and the dive was shorter for everyone.

When planning your dive, you need to take into account the minimum amount of air that you feel happy with having at the end of your 'bottom time'. When you are learning to dive, your instructor gives you very clear instructions on this before the dive. For example, Gérald would ask us to let him know, with one of the underwater signals, when we were down to 100 bars, and then again at 50 bars. Once the first diver got down to 50 bars, the dive would finish and we would all start our ascent. He knew that 50 bars would be enough for us to ascend slowly and do our 3-minute safety stop.

Despite having got off to a crawling start, once I put the theory into practice, it did begin to make sense. As time went by (I can hardly bear to admit this bit), I even actually began to enjoy it. The one thing I found was that it is good to read different books on the various subjects, because sometimes one author can put things in a way that clicks more effectively. I guess there is no incentive like your own safety to inspire you to grasp tricky information and to become a more receptive student.

Getting up quick

And on that issue, one of the theoretical lessons which I found particularly comforting having put it into practice was 'the controlled emergency swimming ascent'. I had found myself on my first few dives looking up at the surface when I was at about 10 meters and thinking, 'I know that I have to come up slowly and do my 3 minute stop at 5 metres, but what if I couldn't? What if I didn't have enough air or I really had to get up because some great big dangerous fish was after me?'

Well the fact is that if you are, for example, completely out of air and your buddy is too, or for some reason you have become separated, then you *can* come up more rapidly if you absolutely have to without blasting your lungs to pieces.

The way to do it is to look up, start swimming to the surface and literally exhale gently all the way up. It is a bit spooky doing it at first because your natural reaction is to want to breathe in or to hold your breath. Once you have the hang of it though, it does make you feel as though you are in more control of your own destiny, should you run into a ghastly out-of-air situation.

On one of my trips to Mauritius, when I first met Mat and Maz, they were completing their 'rescue' course. You can take this once you have done your 'beginners' and 'advanced' courses (PADI call theirs the 'open water' course and the 'advanced' course, CMAS call theirs CMAS Level 1 and Level 2). On the 'rescue' course you learn techniques for rescuing other divers and, as I was to find out when doing it myself, it teaches you how to rescue yourself as well.

On the 'rescue' course, I repeated this exercise. Out of all the exercises I have learnt, I think this is the one which has given me the most confidence. I know that if I absolutely have to, while not ideal, I can get up if all my air sources go kaput.

How not to get lost

The other really useful skill you have to get to grips with when starting off on your basic scuba training is navigation. It won't come as any surprise to you by now to learn that compass reading has never been my forte. I was the only teenager who got lost during their Bronze Duke of Edinburgh course at our school, because I couldn't make out which way to go. Thankfully, one of our geography teachers who was running the course had a motorbike and, after scouring the South Downs of Sussex, finally found me: cold, tired but still maintaining the drama was all caused by a faulty compass, not of course, my lack of reading skills.

It is amazing what you can learn, however, when you realise that it really is a question of survival. No motorbikes are likely to zoom up and rescue you if you get lost on your dive. One of the things which often happens when you lose your way underwater is that apparently you start swimming in circles. Not little ones that are immediately obvious, but big ones, which are really disorientating.

I've only ever dived with Gérald or Thierry, the owner of Sun Divers, and so I've never got lost. I stick to them like glue and they always know where they are going. But I'm glad that my scuba course made me grasp the basics. It really is vital to be able to swim in a straight line and at least start heading for the boat or shore, with the aid of a compass. Not having dived in the murky gravel pits that Mat and Maz have described or in water with poor visibility, I have not actually experienced just how crucial being able to navigate well underwater is. I am told, however, that when you dive in such conditions, you pretty soon become a master at it.

But the main thing I have learnt about scuba diving so far is that you never stop learning. I am never going to make it to being an instructor, but however bumpily I started off I've managed, through grit and determination, to get my head round some subjects that I'd never even grasped before. And perhaps most importantly, I have learnt a very, very healthy respect for this sport and everyone who teaches it.

Chapter 6

Buddy love

The standard definition of a 'buddy' is a good friend, a companion ... you get the picture. This may explain why Bill Clinton named his yummy brown Labrador (who he acquired when the humans all around him were displaying less than kindly intentions) 'Buddy'. Heaven knows he needed a faithful mate to help him through the bad times and to enjoy the good. When it comes to diving, your buddy has a similar although rather more expansive role. One of the most important safety steps you can take is to make sure that you have a red hot buddy because, as already mentioned, your life can literally depend on it.

In diving, your buddy is your diving partner and the person to whom you are meant to stay close by at all times while underwater: you look out for each other's safety throughout the dive. This process begins before you get anywhere near the water. You may plan your dive with your buddy (although this is done for you in lots of dive centres), working out together where you are going, for how long and at what depth, and so on. You familiarise yourselves with each other's equipment before the dive – where your alternate air supplies are, for example – and check that it is all in working order.

Ideally your buddy is someone you know very well and who you dive with regularly. However, it could be someone on whom you have never set eyes before, which can happen when on a diving holiday. No matter how you come to be together or the stage you are at in your diving career, it is really important to take the whole buddying business seriously. Just by checking each other's kit (in addition to having checked your own) you may throw up something simple, such as the fact that you are walking away from the diving centre without your fins, or discovering that a strap on your mask is a bit dodgy or that your tank hasn't been properly filled with air. It always helps to have a second pair of eyes checking things over. This may seem a bit invasive if you don't know the person very well and they start nosing around in your kit, but there is no point in getting uppity. First, you get the chance to do it back, and second, and obviously most crucially, they may pick up a problem that will save you from an accident later in the dive.

Buddy checklist

Once you get to the site of your dive, you can be of real practical help to each other by assisting one another in getting into all the gear – say, manoeuvring the BCD and tank into the right place or handing over fins and making sure they are on comfortably. Since buddying is a two-way process, you both benefit. PADI have a checklist of things to go through with your buddy before diving known as 'BWRAF'. Each initial of BWRAF (which I remember by thinking 'Brave Women of the Royal Air Force') stands for a vital part of the checklist.

The B stands for BCD. You need to check that all the fastenings are secure on your BCD, that the hoses are all in the right position and that the alternate air supply is securely in place. It is also vital to check that the 'rapid purge' on the shoulder is working and that the cord for it is accessible and not trapped under the shoulder strap of your BCD. You pull this to slow you down if you are ascending too quickly and if it is not easy to locate on your BCD then you could be in real trouble. Or you may see your buddy ascending too rapidly and need to give their rapid purge a yank to slow them down. It is also important to check that the 'direct system' (the inflator and deflator hose) is working so you can inflate and deflate the BCD easily. The tank needs to be correctly fitted. If it's too loose, it may fall off.

The W stands for weights. It is important to check that you and your buddy have the correct number of weights, that they are evenly distributed on the weight belt and that they can be quickly and easily released should this become necessary during the dive. It is especially important to familiarise yourself with the weight belts if you are using borrowed equipment from a dive centre.

R is for releases. This means that you both need to know where each other's releases are so that you can easily remove your buddy's BCD should you need to do so when underwater or at the surface. Some BCDs have weight systems built in and some have different types of clasps, so you need to be sure you know how your buddy's BCD works.

A is for air. You need to be sure that you and your buddy both have enough air for your dive as you have planned it and that your valves are open. You have to know in a jiffy where the alternative regulator is and how to access it easily should you need to. It's a bit late to be scrabbling around underwater trying to work it out.

Finally there is F, which is the 'Final OK' that you give each other before entering the water. This involves making sure that there is definitely no missing gear and that things are not dangling around that should be fastened and, rather crucially, that once your gear is all present and correct, that your buddy is actually feeling OK within themselves and wants to dive.

Care and concern

Buddies are supposed to signal to you to enquire about how much air you have left and if you are feeling OK so don't think they are questioning your diving skills or are checking up on you because they do not rate you as a diver. You should be reciprocating the concern throughout the dive to ensure that all is well with them too, every 7–8 minutes, with all else being well. If both of you know how deep you have planned to go, where and for how long you will be down, plus the length of safety stops, you have double the chance of sticking to it all. If all goes to plan, then the dive will be successful. You will go up at the pre-arranged time and with the right amount of air in your tank, and you will make the appropriate safety stops on your ascent. At the end of the dive you can help each other to 'get your kit off', so to speak, and chat about what you've seen.

This is another good thing about having a buddy. As well as looking out for each other, it is a great way to maximise the enjoyment of your time underwater. I've had many a buddy nudge me to show me a fish or coral or ray or turtle swimming in the distance that I would have totally missed had they not given me a prod. Equally, I think I've done the same a few times although I tend to get a bit embarrassed because I find weird things such as the smallest, most teeny insy winsy bit of coral all-consumingly fascinating, and I don't think this is very normal. But you get the idea.

So, a good buddy can really add to the enjoyment of your dive because they can help you to stay calm before going into the water (because you know you have checked and double-checked safety and the dive plan), can show you stuff you may otherwise have missed, and can have a great chinwag with you about it all afterwards.

Confidence if things go wrong

Also, and crucially, you can help each other out if things do *not* go to plan during your dive. This is why it is so important that you remain close by each other. It is hard to help if one of you has gone off on your own. I have never been in a situation, thank heavens, where a buddy or I have run out of air, but I have seen it happen. This is where your very first bit of training springs automatically into action and you get on with the business of sharing the air supply of the diver who does still have air through their spare regulator and alternate air source. This automatically means that the dive is at the end and, once you have sorted your breathing out using the alternative air source, you both ascend slowly and carefully so that you both have the best chance of reaching the surface in safety. The calmer you remain, the less heavily you breathe, the less air you use, and the more you have to share to get you to the surface. I don't suppose it's easy to remain completely cool and unphased in these situations, but it certainly helps if you are able to conquer your nerves and deal with the situation in the least stressy way possible. Having confidence in your buddy can help make this possible.

Buddies can also help with practical problems underwater. I know of divers who have accidentally become entangled in a bit of old rope lurking on the seabed. Their buddies were able to free them. If they had been diving on their own, a serious problem might have arisen. In another, especially alarming tale, Gérald told me of a diver who went deeper than he should because he became 'narced'.

Nitrogen narcosis is a clinical syndrome that is characterised by brain, nerve and muscle control going haywire because too much nitrogen is building up in the body. In essence, it can lead to changes in mood, behaviour and perceptions. Some people get really high (what Jacques Cousteau called 'rapture of the deep') and they lose their sense of responsibility. This particular diver was heading downwards at a rapid rate of knots, much to the alarm of his fortunately 'un-narced' buddy, who realised that he wasn't responding to the signals to stop descending. The buddy acted quickly, grabbing him and stopping his descent into oblivion. The narced diver didn't appreciate it at all at the time, because his perceptions were right up the Swanee, but he changed his tune when back on dry land, where he realised that his buddy had saved him from Davey Jones's locker.

A bad buddy

While none of these difficulties have ever happened to me, I did once have a buddy who didn't take a jot of notice of the dive our instructor had planned for us. He told us specifically to stay with him, but my buddy just shot off in all directions, doing exactly as she pleased. I wasn't sure whether to stay with her (she was my alternative source of air after all should anything have gone wrong for me), or to stay in proximity to the instructor as we had been directed to do on the boat. I kept trying to get her to come back to the group, but she ignored me and went on her own sweet way. I began to swim back to the group because I was getting worried. My best interests definitely were not close to her heart, and, at risk of telling tales, I thought I'd better let the instructor know what was going on. When he saw me swimming away from my buddy, I got an underwater roasting with pretty firm gesticulations, which I realised meant, 'Why aren't you with her?' Not being an expert in sign language it was hard to 'reply' with, 'Because she keeps leaving me on my tod and, frankly, she's putting me in danger because she doesn't give a fig about my safety, has forgotten she is a mere mortal and not amphibious, and I'd rather be close to you who does care rather than to her, as she is clearly a total nutter.' Somehow I got the vague gist of it across, and he shot off and gave her the dressing down she deserved. I didn't gloat because that's not what it was all about. I just wanted to know that my buddy was doing her bit for our joint safety.

Octopus's garden

I suppose this isn't a very sensible thing to mention, given that by virtue of your reading this book, you may be of a nervous disposition when it comes to diving, but I think I learnt a lot from hearing other people's stories. If nothing else, they teach you what not to do. So I won't apologise for telling you the following buddy story, which involves a fairly newly qualified dive master, a normally docile octopus and, thankfully, a big brute of a buddy.

The octopus was a regular attraction on this particular dive site. The dive master in question often pointed it out to his clients. On this particular day, wanting to impress them, he got a bit closer than normal. The octopus wasn't too happy about the intrusion, whipped out from behind its rock and clamped itself firmly on top of the diver's head. With its strong thick tentacles it swiftly knocked off the diver's mask, grabbed the regulator out of his mouth and began

wrapping itself around his neck. Every time the diver released himself from the vice-like grip of one tentacle, the octopus just replaced it with another. No problem, it had eight to choose from, after all. Enter the supersonic buddy who literally yanked the octopus by its head off the diver's head, and just in time. The clients had certainly been entertained, but not in the way expected. Air supply restored, it became clear that the octopus was a she and had been in the process of laying her eggs behind her rock. No wonder she got the hump.

Extra set of eyes

If you see your buddy looking like they may touch the local wildlife, do what you need to signal them not to. This saved me from a nasty fate when I was being pushed by a small current, quite unwittingly, towards a stone fish. Stone fish are so well disguised that it can be tricky to see them. By pointing it out, my buddy averted a nasty and venomous sting that has been known to finish divers off. If it doesn't do this while you are underwater, it can do so by causing gangrene and amputations. Stone fish are not aggressive, they just react and defend themselves if you touch them. Because you are looking in one direction when you dive, forwards, it is sometimes hard to see things to your sides. You and your buddy can help by being the other's extra set of eyes.

As well as checking for each other's air, making sure you both stick to your dive plans, averting problems and helping each other with any that do arise, you may also be able to make the dive more pleasant by being observant. If, for example, you see your buddy constantly clearing their mask, it could be simply that they have got some hair stuck in it. A quick once-over and a gentle pull to dislodge the hair may be all that's required for them to continue with a more enjoyable dive.

Lots of people like to dive with the same buddy. Rather than familiarity breeding contempt, knowing your buddy really well can give a great sense of security and confidence. On the other hand, you have to be extra sure that you do not fall into the old cliché of becoming overly familiar and forgetting to take the whole dive-planning and BWRAF-checking thing really seriously.

There are times when familiarity may hold other hidden problems. My friend Jane said that she'd definitely rather not dive with her hubby if they'd just had a row. 'The last thing you need when diving is the thought lurking in the back of your mind that they'd rather see you sink than swim! On the other hand, I do know that he takes his fitness and weight really seriously, so it's unlikely that he's going to peg out with a coronary or something awful.'

Staying in good nick

That may sound a little on the dramatic side but, as I have already mentioned briefly, it seems to be one thing that is easy to forget when diving. As with other sports, you do need to keep in shape. It's not as obvious as with, say, squash, where carrying excess weight will clearly slow you down on the court. But if you are a diver and are carrying excess weight, the consequences may, for a variety of reasons, put you and your buddy at risk. Obesity, for instance, ups your chances of having raised cholesterol and high blood pressure. Both put an extra strain on your blood's circulation and may increase the risk of having a heart attack or stroke when underwater. It can also mean that you get out of puff more quickly and use up your air more rapidly under normal diving conditions. No one is saying that overweight people should not dive, but we all owe it to our buddies to be as safe as possible under water, so we need to be in good nick physically. Getting a regular check-up from your GP is a responsible thing to do if you dive regularly and is perhaps even more so if you know that you are carrying excess weight. When you meet your buddy for the first time at a diving centre, then obviously it would be the height of rudeness to turn round and say, 'I'm not diving with you, mate! You're a bit on the lardy side for my liking.' But if you feel worried about any aspect of your buddy's apparent state of health or lack of it – if they smell of booze from the night before, for example – then you may want to discreetly tell the person in charge of your dive and let them deal with the tricky situation. However, if you still do not like the outcome, then it is your right to look after your own safety by speaking out.

As for your own health, it is up to you to be realistic and responsible about it. The whole buddy business is about looking out for each other. You can't start throwing your weight around, however much that may be, about anyone else's health if you are not responsible about your own, and you owe it to everyone you are diving with to be as good a buddy as possible, in every possible way.

The Waltons of the underwater world

While the buddy system is to be followed with due care and respect, I have heard of some instances where people get a little over enthusiastic about the 'looking out for each other' rules of diving.

Christoph Pelicier is one of the most respected divers in Mauritius, an instructor of the very highest calibre who runs his own dive center called Abyss. On the basis that it is always best to ensure that your clients feel at ease in the water, he decided to agree to one Norwegian family's request – to have a rope joining them all together on their dive. This was how they always dived *en famille* in the familiar and very low-visibility waters of their home country.

In spite of Christoph gently explaining that 'vis' (as divers say) is excellent in the Indian Ocean – most days you can see for miles around – there was no persuading the father. He wanted a family umbilical cord and that was that.

Off they went to the boat, out to the dive site and over the side of the boat they back-rolled, all five of them immediately attaching themselves with quick-release clips to a long length of rope like a set of charms on a bracelet. The dive went smoothly, Christoph hiding his incredulity at the sight of the Mum and offspring all apparently happy to follow wherever Dad chose to lead them.

But there was one hairy moment when Christoph tried to show them an anemone with a clown fish. Dad came round on one side of Christoph to take a look while Mum came round from the other. The kids who were behind him were unsurprisingly jostling for position to get a good look, too, and in so doing nearly strangled Christoph with their rope. Oops!

CHAPTER 7

Rocks, wrecks and coral orgies

There is no question that many divers I've chatted with find the underwater world of fish, whacking great turtles, rays, octopuses, eels and lobsters an endlessly stimulating environment in which to find themselves. The way the sea creatures look, move and behave is utterly captivating and the colours, as I have endlessly droned on, are something to behold. No doubt you have grasped this by now.

But there is another aspect to diving about which Gérald sparked my interest when he mentioned the word 'Cathedral' to me after my very first dive. 'I'm going to take you to one of our dive sites called the Cathedral,' I recalled him saying. He had described it as being a large, mostly open cave into which light simply pours. I distinctly remember him telling me that every time he goes there, despite seeing it hundreds of times before, he is still dumbstruck by its beauty. 'Sometimes I have to deliberately stop my jaw dropping, which would be a natural reaction, were I on land, in the presence of this sight. But that's how it feels when I see it. The Cathedral is, quite simply, an enduringly, jaw-droppingly, beautiful rock structure.'

Since learning to dive, I have found being in the presence of such rock structures to be yet another of the wonderful thrills that come with this sport. Massive rock faces, drop-offs and arches can be as fascinating as the fish. Lucky for me that I feel this way, given that much of my diving experience has been in Mauritius, an island that was formed by volcanic activity over 12 million years ago. Although there have been no volcanic rumblings on the island for over 100,000 years, the evidence of its geographical origins are everywhere you look. On land, there are broken rings of mountain ranges, some up to 800 metres above sea level. And underwater, the island's volcanic past has left its mark on the marvellous rock formations that lie beyond its ring of coral reefs and shallow lagoons.

Defying gravity

One day, when diving down the edge of a great big rock face, I remembered something I'd heard from Gérald. He said that when you go down and – later on at the end of the dive – back up again, it is like being in an elevator ... but without the elevator. I can see exactly what he means: suspended in the water, you can move like Peter Pan in a pantomime, minus the ropes that allow him to 'fly'. This must be how Spiderman would feel. Or Batman and Robin for that matter. There is no gravity keeping you down so you can glide around pretending that you have defied that one law of physics even I understand.

There is an especially good site called the Canyon off the west coast of Mauritius, where it feels like you are zooming along inside the Grand Canyon in mid-air, pretending that your air tank is actually a rocket-charged backpack powering you along. It never ceases to amaze me when we surface from this particular dive and I hear other divers moaning on about the fact there were not many fish around. I feel like saying, 'But didn't you feel like you were Catwoman?' but I know the blank looks that would be the response so I keep it to myself. Anyway, we all enjoy different things and rocks are obviously not their thing. Gérald knows what I mean though.

Geological wonders

The thrill for me is easy to trace. I absolutely loved physical geography lessons at school and if I hadn't become a nutritionist would certainly have taken the geological path in life. I found it astonishing how land masses were created through glaciation and volcanic eruptions. I loved walking in the Lake District on school field trips and seeing for myself the 'U-shaped valleys' and 'truncated spurs' formed by massive flows of ice surging across our landscapes. And when walking down the Royal Mile in Edinburgh I was far more fascinated by the fact that the castle is built on a volcanic plug than interested in peering in the shops.

As well as enormous rock faces below sea level, there are also amazing arches, some of which resemble underwater versions of the Arc de Triomphe. They are great fun to swim through, too, although the small ones freaked me out a bit at first. The big ones, however, I have always found to be terribly theatrical. Coming through one large arch on a site called Roche Zo Zo on the south-east coast of Mauritius, with Gérald waiting to take a photograph as I appeared, my torch in hand, I could not help but feel a sense of occasion, as though on stage at the London Palladium with the curtains being raised.

Arches and rock faces have this special way of making me feel very small, giving me a sense of perspective about life. Like Stonehenge in Salisbury, the pyramids in Egypt or even an old oak tree, they have been around for so much longer than me and will still be there, way after I have rejoined the carbon and nitrogen cycle. 'If I'm having a bad day, if someone is getting to me,' Gérald told me while we were chatting recently, 'I love to glide among the gigantic rock structures. Bathed in the soft blue light, which is so much kinder on your eyes, I can guarantee to be able to put some order back in my brain, to prioritise the important things in life, to give less value to the unimportant and to shake off the annoyances that inevitably come with everyday living. The rocks have an energy, a presence. A way to diffuse stress and rebalance your mind.'

Life on the rock face

As you are gliding around the rock faces there is a surprisingly wide range of life attached to their surfaces that you can observe. Some of the big clams holding on for dear life look as though they have army fatigues on the frilly fleshy bits that you can see when they are open. Get just that tiny bit too close and they react with the speed of any well-trained military man, snapping themselves safely shut within the blink of an eye, their shells blending in perfectly with the rock on which they are perched.

And it is fascinating to see what look like pretty bright blue and purple flowers disappearing in on themselves. They are in fact tiny little tubular worms, which retract within a split second of you getting too close. I have also found that it is well worth stopping to take a look at coral-like 'sticks' that grow out from rock faces. If you look really carefully you might be lucky enough to also see a regular inhabitant, the transparent dwarf goby fish, which dashes up and down the 'twig' like a frantic shuttle bus.

Scary caves and wonderful wrecks

All this said, there is one part of rocks and their structures that I know I wouldn't enjoy exploring and that is the real caves. It comes back, I think, to always acknowledging your limitations. As much as I enthuse over how wonderful the general experience of recreational diving can be, if you absolutely categorically know something is beyond your comfort zone, then that is how it is. In my view, it is not worth fighting.

Much as I'm happy to walk up Old Man Coniston in the Lake District, wild horses would not drag me down into one of its pot holes. Similarly, as much as I love 'scaling' the enormous rock faces, whizzing in and out of arches and being transfixed by the joy of entering open-ended caves, I just know that true cave diving is not for me, although lots of divers I have met are hooked on their caving experiences.

Wrecks, on the other hand, can add another dimension to the kind of day's dive I get a kick from. I have never dived in England, but apparently wrecks around the coast can be absorbing. I must admit when I saw my first wreck, in spite of the fact that it was a tug that had been deliberately sunk to help create an artificial reef and had no heroic associations of a captain standing at the helm, ensuring all his crew left before him, as his vessel plunged towards the ocean floor, it was hard not to wonder who had trodden its decks, how many journeys it had made and through which seas this sturdy vessel had ploughed its way during its working life.

As I was gliding up the staircase on a recent wreck dive, moving up to the front of the ship where the balustrade on the bow was completely intact, it did not require much imagination to envision Leonardo DiCaprio holding on to Kate Winslet as her russet locks flowed out behind her. As I was humming (you can hum into your regulator, honestly) the tune to Celine Dion's 'My Heart Will Go On', the classic that accompanied that particular scene in the movie *Titanic*, the current, which was a bit strong that day, suddenly blew me off course. I finned back down to the foredeck, where my buddy popped all my romantic musings as he pointed out the bathroom of the sailors, toilet half intact.

I always get such a special, 'being in on a secret'-type feeling when I see a wreck. I can only begin to imagine how it must feel actually to discover one, or how the marine biologists and oceanographic experts working with the director James Cameron must have felt when lowered in special deep ocean submersibles to extraordinary depths to get the footage for *The Real Titanic*.

A wreck of a home

Whether the wreck you are diving to is in shallow tropical waters or the colder seas surrounding the UK, one of the most exhilarating moments is when you are able to gradually make out its form as you dive towards its resting place on the ocean bed. Then, as you get closer, it becomes possible to make out not just the structure, but also the way in which the adaptable marine life has quickly made a home from the new addition to its environment.

I have a favourite wreck in Mauritius which is home to two wild-looking leaf fish. These leaf fish like to loiter, swaying in the soft movement of the water, appearing for all the world to be bits of straggly orange seaweed. They seem to love it there. And as you swim over its deck you can often see a massive moray eel poking out from the old deck vent where it has taken up residence.

As with all diving, the rule is to Look Not Touch, to follow the instructions of the local divers and to stick to the safety rules at all times. The last thing you want to do is to put your arm into a porthole and pull it out with a stung, bitten or chopped-off hand, to get yourself snagged or cut on bits of rusted metal or snared in ropes. It is also wise to bear in mind that as water moves through a wreck it can create suction and surges that could pull you where you don't want to be pulled. Because many wrecks are not close to the shore but are in deeper water, you usually only get to see them once your diving has progressed a certain amount, or after you have done some specialist training or at least some reading about the special considerations.

Wrecks, whether deliberately sunk or not, can become a new habitat for corals as well as all kinds of fish and other marine creatures, and it lifts your spirits when you see a new piece of coral that has decided to use a balustrade as a place on which to form its new home. I admit to having had virtually no knowledge of corals before taking to the oceans kitted up with scuba gear. I'd swum over some on the reef while learning to snorkel again, but they looked like odd-shaped bits of little tiny rocks. What I have discovered is a clear example of when ignorance is definitely not bliss.

Classes in corals

Swotting up on what coral is and how it forms has been a riveting journey and I still know virtually nothing in the grand scheme of things. People, I have discovered, devote their entire lives to studying coral around the world and it is just as well, because the more they can tell us about it, the more people may get off their bottoms and begin doing something to help preserve it.

Far from being an inanimate piece of stone or rock, coral is alive, though not literally kicking, and needs, like us, good 'nutrition'. Each tiny coral polyp – a spineless animal – requires sunlight, warm temperatures and a salty environment. Related to jellyfish and anemones, a polyp can be as small as 0.01 millimetres and has a sac-like body and a mouth that is surrounded by stinging tentacles. It cleverly uses the calcium carbonate from seawater to build itself a hard, cup-shaped limestone skeleton (rather like we use the calcium in milk to make our bones). This tough skeleton then protects the delicate body of the polyp. Different types of coral polyp feed themselves in slightly different ways. Many have algae living in them that use the sunlight to make carbohydrates, which supplies the polyp with calories. The algae takes the polyp's waste, which it uses as a source of nutrients for itself and to make oxygen for the polyp. The algae get the benefit of a safe 'roof' over their head. It's a real two-way relationship, each benefiting from the other. Alternatively, other corals wait until night-time and then pop out their tentacles to catch tiny, tiny little animals known as 'zooplankton' that are floating by. The polyps sting their prey, then gobble them down to be digested in their stomachs.

Each mound of branching coral that you may see when you dive is a whole load of these animals and their skeletons bunched together in a colony. While wrecks provide an attachment place for the polyps to make their bony homes, they are better known for forming reefs around, for example, islands like Mauritius and its neighbouring sister island Rodrigues.

Coral reefs are massive and intricate structures. Some contain living polyps, some are left behind when the polyps die and become the foundations for new polyps that build their skeletons on top, rather like a high-rise block of flats. In fact, these foundations can also be composed of the remains of various algae, sponges, clams, seaweed and mud. It seems incredible to me that something that appears to be a piece of rock is actually made of layer upon layer of tiny skeletons covered by a thin layer of living polyps busily constructing the next layer.

Coral conservation

One of the things that really made me want to get my buoyancy well under control was the huge desire not to go crashing into bits of coral, especially on finding out that they grow on average between just 5 and 25 millimetres in length per year. The last thing they need is a clumsy fin of mine to smash 10 years' work to smithereens in just a second. It's their world after all in which, as divers, we are just passing visitors.

Coral can be astonishingly diverse and, like so much of the underwater world, breathtakingly beautiful. Although there are many hundreds of various species of coral, I found it easiest to grasp the simple classification of 'hard' and 'soft' versions. The hard ones are the ones I've just described. They grow in colonies and are the makers of coral reefs. They form an absolute plethora of shapes from flattened versions to those that have hard points like stalagmites. Soft corals can often be mistaken for plants and

can even look a bit like trees. Instead of making limestone skeletons for themselves, they grow wood-like cores for structural support and fleshy rinds for protection. These soft corals do not build reefs but instead can form themselves into gigantic 'sea fans' which sway in the current. Diving through a forest of sea fans is yet another diving treat. These majestic see-through fan-shaped corals bend and sway with the movement of the water, bowing in reverence before you like servants fanning members of the imperial family in an ancient Chinese court.

When I was lucky enough to find myself diving in Rodrigues, I found myself finning above and around such a diverse range of hard corals that even now I can see them clearly in my mind's eye. The range of colours is imprinted as well as the variety of shapes. Just a few metres below the surface it was as if I was entering a prize-winning country garden in a flower show. It was quite overwhelming, and hard to know where to look first. Some were like dusky pinkish mushrooms, others like big yellow flowers. There were purple clusters of branching corals and some that looked like creamy comfy duvets. I spotted tanned leather-like coral slung over a large rock that looked like a cowboy's saddle, green 'brain' coral, which, as its name suggests, looks spookily like the surface of our brains and also, more appetisingly, pristine white corals shaped like tables ready to be set for afternoon tea. This artist's palette of colours comes from the pigment-producing algae living inside the transparent bodies of the polyps. Since several million algae can live within a couple of centimetres squared of coral, it is easy to see how they bring such vibrancy to reefs.

According to a recent report from the American Association for the Advancement of Science, Rodrigues is listed fourth among the world's 10 most important reef areas. It is also a favourite diving destination of Prince William, who it has been said, made the study of Rodriguan corals part of his degree dissertation. Certainly locals are discreet yet immensely proud of their royal connection.

The joy of sex

While the massive variety of shapes, forms and colours are always on show when you venture underwater in coral-building oceans, one aspect of a coral's life that you would be beyond lucky to catch is their process of reproduction. They actually do it in a variety of ways depending on the species, but the method that fascinated me most was described by Benoit, the owner of Bouba Diving on the south-east coast of Rodrigues.

Benoit told us that, once a year, there is the possibility of doing a 'boy's only' dive. It is rare to catch this annual event, which takes place at the end of September to the beginning of October. You have to be there on precisely the right night, which is slightly down to luck and slightly down to Benoit's judgement. 'The corals literally throw their sperm around,' enthused Benoit, 'it's really not a sight for girls.'

What he was describing was how some coral eject trillions of sperm and eggs into the surrounding water, creating a massive reproductive jamboree known, somewhat conservatively, as 'coral spawning'. As the Coral Reef Alliance, a body dedicated to preserving coral, observes, 'It is one of the most astounding acts of synchronicity in the natural world.' I agree that it would be just astounding to witness it. Once fertilised, the larvae swim to the surface of the sea. If not eaten by fish, they then sink back down, attach themselves to a hard surface and transform themselves into a coral polyp.

Other corals are more discreet in their reproductive methods. Some are hermaphrodites, producing both sperm and eggs. Others form boys-only and girls-only single-sex

Rocks, wrecks and coral orgies **99**

colonies and manage to cross-colonise in fairly unflamboyant ways.

Coral reefs provide a home to a massive number of reef fish and plants, a quarter of all known marine species, as well as being fascinatingly beautiful to observe in their own right. Because they can be close to the surface, coral reefs are a great way of easing yourself into the wonders of the underwater world. If you are fascinated by what you see when you snorkel above them, they may be just the incentive you need to take the next step to be able to scuba-dive among them, getting up close for a really good ogle.

Under threat

But you had better get a move on. Corals are being destroyed at this very moment all around the world through the effects of pollution from harmful fertilisers and waste from oil and gas production. As levels of nitrogen in our waters increase, algae growth booms and cuts off the corals' sunlight. Not only this, but the sediments that run off from factories can also block out the crucial source of sunlight and can kill off reefs by smothering them in their gunk. Coastal development and sewage dumped directly into the seas can also rapidly break down reefs, while destructive fishing practices such as cyanide and blast fishing utterly destroys corals. And of course there is also global warming, caused by the build-up of carbon dioxide trapping heat in the atmosphere and warming the environment and, as many marine experts believe, the surface of certain seas as well, to the point where the coral dies. Bleaching occurs, where the colourful algae inside the polyps of coral can no longer survive, making the coral turn white and often dying in the process.

Fortunately there are organisations around the world who are striving to preserve coral reefs and to bring to wider public attention the current dangers that threaten them. Probably the best known coral reef in the world is the Great Barrier Reef. When you hear that marine scientists predict that this tremendous wonder of the world could lose most of its coral cover by the middle of this century, it kind of puts the gravity of the situation into perspective.

Thank goodness divers can be of real help. You can, for example, join a group like Reef Check. Since it began in 1996, Reef Check (a member of the International Coral Alliance) has developed into the biggest volunteer programme monitoring coral reefs and is now active in more than 60 countries. By joining the 5,000 plus volunteer divers who have been trained in Reef Check methods, you can learn how to help monitor sites, educate Joe Bloggs about the current problems facing reefs and help local communities sustain their livelihoods, which rely on the coral reefs.

I'm not just banging on like an overly zealous environmental campaigner. One of the things that diving has made me become aware of and reflect on is the need to start taking our waterways, from lakes and rivers to seas and oceans, a lot more seriously than we do right now. Many people around the world can do this much more eloquently and knowledgably than I. But it seems so incredibly obvious that a lack of respect, understanding and action now will not only kill off the lovely things that, as a diver, you could have the opportunity of witnessing, but could also change life as we know it, for us and future generations everywhere, both in and out of the water.

CHAPTER 8

'Most sharks are vegetarian'

I know, I know, you would have to be really gullible –
great whites aside, who we *all* know eat everything from
cute penguins to us – to believe that most sharks are
vegetarian. But there are times when ignorance is bliss, and
when one experienced diver told me that most sharks are, in
fact, vegetarian, I felt a lot happier about the whole
'sharkophobia' business. Quite what I thought those great
beasts of the oceans survived on I really don't know, but as I
began to think it through, the idea that they may prefer the
marine-life version of a feta cheese salad to, say, my right
leg, stopped making sense, even to me.

I began my research into sharks with the 'know thine
enemy' approach in mind, believing it was better to try and
understand these creatures and to get to the bottom of
their real risk to divers than to flap around, terrified, in the
unknown. I bought about 50 books on the subject and, lo
and behold, there is no such thing as a herbivorous shark.
Not one. Of the 500 plus species circulating in our global
waters, they are all hardened meat eaters although, it has to
be said, the tiger shark, for instance, is not the most
discerning of diners, having been found with all sorts of
things from beer bottles to shoes (don't even think about it),
dogs, cats, cans of salmon and peas and even bags of
potatoes and coal in their stomachs.

I've always loathed those marine biologist types who,
on the back of a report in a newspaper about some poor

surfer being gobbled up as an afternoon snack by a great white off an idyllic paradise beach bleat on about the shark being 'more hunted than the hunter'. Yeah, right. I'm not sure that's what the surfer was thinking at the moment they realised their time was up as the teeth sunk into their flesh, or, indeed how their family may have felt after the event. Yet the more I read, the more I could see that they had a point. As Michael Bright, author of *The Private Life of Sharks*, tells us, there are more deaths from car accidents in one month than all recorded fatal shark attacks ever, but we get into cars most days of our lives without giving the dangers a second thought. That said, when you dig a bit deeper into the statistic, maybe there would be as many deaths from shark attacks if the same number of people that drive cars every day swam in areas of high shark populations. I'm no statistician, so I don't know. Maybe it is a bit of an unrealistic comparison, but it is at least a starting point for getting the number of shark attacks that have taken place, according to the researchers, into perspective.

Would you rather a bee or a shark?

According to some sources, attacks by great whites are increasing, but it might be better, rather than comparing the total number of shark attacks with the total number of car accidents, to realise that bees, wasps and snakes actually finish off more of us each year with their stings and bites than do sharks. And just for good measure, you are more likely to die of a heart attack or from drowning when swimming close to the shore than from a shark attack. Even so, our imaginations run riot with the very thought of being pulled down, gasping for air and life while clamped in the jaws of a terrifyingly powerful shark. It is probably because we are so very out of control when in the water, added to the gory way in which a shark might rip us apart and wolf us down, that makes it all seem such an awful way to meet our end.

When it comes to sharks and scuba-diving, it is hard to say that you are at much more risk than when paddling or swimming in the shallows on a beach. According to the International Shark Attack File, which has the gory duty of logging shark attacks around the world, of the 1,406 recorded attacks that have taken place since the mid-1800s, half were on swimmers at the surface or on people wading in shallow water. When trying to get a sense of perspective on the whole issue of shark attacks, another thing to bear in mind is that they take place in a wide variety of places. They may happen in daylight or in the dark, in open seas or shallow seas, at the mouths of rivers or in narrow rivers leading to the sea, and attacks have been recorded all over the world in waters of all temperatures. That said, according to the Collins field guide *Sharks of the World*, many attacks tend to occur near dawn or dusk, when sharks are hunting actively. And many happen in murky water, such as at the mouths of rivers, after a lot of rain or during onshore winds. The poor visibility caused by these situations seems more likely to lead to cases of mistaken identity, with a smaller shark going for a bite and chomping you rather than its preferred prey. Bigger sharks can use the poor visibility to their advantage by getting closer to you before you realise they are there, so you have less chance to escape.

What not to do

As the field guide points out, the number of attacks on humans has not increased proportionally to the increased number of us taking up water sports when on holiday to hot destinations. They also point out that there are quite a few things that we can do to reduce the chances of provoking an attack and, obviously, I read this particular section with heightened concentration. There seems to be a quite simple 'What Not To Do' set of guidelines that will reduce your own chances of becoming a shark-attack victim:

• Avoid swimming erratically and thrashing around in the water. This attracts a shark's attention from miles away.

• Avoid swimming with dolphins. Yes, I know it is the in thing, but you may feel less inclined to join Flipper if you know that dolphins are often accompanied by sharks.

• Avoid swimming alone. Being in a group can make you less of a special target.

• Avoid having a wee-wee in the water. Hold it until you get back to shore.

• Don't feed sharks or spear fish. Feeding them is a bad idea if you want to avoid an attack.

• Don't swim near fishing boats throwing slurry overboard – sharks may be attracted by the 'food'.

• Avoid wearing highly coloured and contrasting clothing.

• Don't follow sharks closely or pull their tails. (As if you would!)

Although it is always worth following these 'What Not To Do' rules to help lower your chances of a shark attack, bear in mind that while sharks go for relatively few people in the total scheme of animal attacks on humans, you cannot specifically narrow them down to any particular place, time, ocean or set of conditions.

In one especially bizarre incident, Bright says that back in 1972 at Taperro Beach near Adelaide in South Australia, a 1.8 metre-long shark (no one managed to identify which type) went for a woman in shallow water. She ran like Billy-o out of the water, as you may expect, and up onto the beach. The shark followed. Luckily for her, she escaped and just kept running up the beach, but the shark couldn't stop either and ended up high and dry on the sand. Good job she was a nifty sprinter. Rather appropriately, this is what is described as a 'hit and run' attack, where the shark has a go at the legs, probably because it thinks that the swimmer is its more usual marine-life type of prey. There is not much you can do about this kind of attack, except hope that you get away with an injury, your life and I assume, in every case, one heck of a dose of shock.

Not in my territory

As a diver, it is more likely that a shark will attack because you have gone into its territory. Under such circumstances, the shark may do a quick preliminary 'slash attack' to warn you off. This gives you time to attempt quietly backing off and to hope that they get the message that you are a friend not a foe before they come in and go for you for real. A 'bump and bite' attack is more of a problem, because the shark is more likely to really bite you. Unfortunately, if you

'Most sharks are vegetarian' **107**

find a shark circling you, then this may be what it's up to. They circle, then come and give you a quick bump to check you out before actually attacking, and there is not a lot you can do about it. The 'sneak' attack is the Jaws-type attack, when the shark comes from below and behind and takes a bite without any warning. Great whites are said to prefer blubber or fatty meat to our leaner bodies, so rather than from being eaten, death can often occur from the person bleeding to death or drowning after the attack.

I suppose the truth is that as a scuba-diver you are implicitly at risk of being attacked by a shark. But you are equally at risk of any number of things that may go wrong when diving, such as using up your air more rapidly than you had thought, bumping inadvertently into a poisonous stone fish or getting separated from your buddy and running into trouble on your tod.

Diving comes with risks and you have to weigh them up before taking the plunge. Forewarned, I believe, is always forearmed, and learning about sharks has certainly helped to quell my fears. Not because I think I could do much to avert a full-on, out-of-the-blue attack, but I have grasped the idea that it is possible to lower your odds by following the 'What Not To Do' behaviour, and know that whether a shark is around is a matter of luck. The odds are that when scuba-diving, if you stick with your dive leader and do not do daft things or dive in places you are advised not to, the chances are that you will be OK.

Facing the fear

I'm not just saying this. From the frightened nine-year-old on the lilo off Bognor beach, I actually found myself saying 'Yes' to diving in a place in Mauritius called 'Shark Point'. This is not a story about heroics, just about how, by changing your point of view, you can learn to face your demons, put them into perspective and find yourself doing things you could never have believed possible.

One of the reasons I decided to go on the trip was because I was with divers who I trusted implicitly. A second was because there had been no known fatalities or attacks during trips to this dive site, which is to see grey-tipped reef sharks – a 'safer' kind of shark to say great white, blue, white-tip, bull, tiger or mako for instance, which are more likely to go for you. The third was because Geri, who I have spent hours chatting away to while she does my hair at John Frieda's in London, had told me wonderful stories about her own experiences of diving with sharks. Her words, 'They are not all man-eaters you know Amanda,' were ringing in my ears as we powered through the massive waves off the north coast of Mauritius to get to the Shark Point dive site. I was nervous, no question. I always get nervous when diving at a new place, from a boat I am not familiar with and having to follow instructions for specific types of entry into the water just in case I get it wrong. The idea of seeing sharks was certainly adding to the tension.

When we arrived underwater at the place where the sharks were usually to be seen, we found ourselves just on the edge of an open-topped 'cave'. We had come in via a side entrance while the sharks had popped in through the open top. The cave was circular and the sharks were swimming round anti-clockwise in the well-oxygenated water. There was a heck of a current, so we had to hold on tightly to rocks to stop being swept into the whooshing circle of water. It was a bit like being at the Royal Albert Hall or in a coliseum-style theatre peering at a circular 'stage'. Round and round they went and seeing them so close that I could reach out and touch them was quite, quite extraordinary.

Their mouths were set with that downwards slant, they looked dangerous, sinister and yet incredibly – dare I even mention the word?– elegant. Yes, they were elegant in both their movements and shape. Here before me were examples of creatures whose body shapes evolved up to 350 million years ago with such a perfect form that it has hardly altered since.

A perfect design

Although it looks really sleek and smooth, shark skin is far from it. In fact, in most cases, it is made up of tiny little tooth-like projections. The roughness this gives the skin reduces drag when the shark swims, allowing it to go faster with less effort. We may soon see Olympic swimmers with costumes designed with a rough rather than smooth surface and even aeroplanes and spacecraft, given that Mother Nature has proven it to be so effective. Talking of Mother Nature, she has done an especially fine job with one particular shark that, when in the shallow waters off Hawaii, is able to produce a pigment in its skin that protects it from excessive ultraviolet radiation and from burning – just as we make melanin in our skin to offer similar protection. Wild isn't it?!

What is obvious to the naked eye though, in the case of the 'cylindrical' rather than flat sharks at least, is the way they move with such extraordinary flexibility and can turn in very tight circles. This is because instead of having a bony skeleton, theirs is made from bendy cartilage. Not only can they move like the clappers, they can also turn really rapidly and swim with a wiggle. The main dorsal fin (which it is hard to even conjure in my mind's eye without an accompanying 'Dah *dah*, dah *dah*, dah *dah*, dah *dah*', from the just-about-to-attack music of the *Jaws* film) is there not to frighten the life out of cinema goers, but to give the shark stability as it swims.

As for the teeth, well, they vary in size and shape depending on the species, but in general they grow extraordinarily rapidly and have multiple rows. I remember a boy at school who, through a quirk of nature, had a couple of rows of teeth and, kids being kids, he was known affectionately as 'Great White' until the orthodontist got to grips with his unusual dentition. In sharks, each row can last a matter of only eight days to several months. A conveyor-belt replacement system, where rows of teeth edge forward to replace those in front as they fall out, is common to them all.

A shark's dinner

With over 500 species, it is hard to generalise, but the teeth tend to be suited to the kind of food that the particular shark usually feeds on, which of course makes utter evolutionary sense. For example, great whites have saw-like teeth in their top jaws to make short work of flesh and bone, while on the bottom they have teeth shaped to keep hold of the prey. Tiger sharks have serrated teeth that are so sharp they can get through the hardened shell of turtles. According to experts, sharks do not really bite with any more force than we humans. It is just that the big boys are so big that the total force is immense.

Not all sharks go around ripping into their food; whale sharks, the largest of all sharks and the biggest fish in the world, just slowly glide along with their mouths open, scooping up floating plankton along with krill, squid and small fish. Given that whale sharks can be as long as the length of two buses, it makes you realise how this diet is clearly extremely nutritious. Basking sharks feed in a similar way, also dining on plankton. They live in cooler waters and are often spotted off the south coast of the UK. These are the ones my Dad was referring to in fact.

Neither the whale shark nor the basking shark pose a threat to us in terms of us ending up in their stomachs. Friends of mine who have swum with whale sharks can hardly find words to describe the experience. Their sheer size seems to take words away from the most verbose. 'Awestruck' seems to sum it up. It certainly was the word Gérald used when he described coming across one off the coast of Flic en Flac. He simply couldn't believe his eyes.

I could almost cut my own fingers off for typing this stuff. Talk about doing a U-turn. But I have to, because of my one experience of seeing those grey-tipped reef sharks, swimming in such close proximity and feeling in no danger at all. Had I been circled and then bumped by a bull shark going for an attack, I have absolutely no doubt whatsoever that my opinion would be very different, but seeing them in this context made it impossible not to be impressed by their physicality.

Bungee jumping of the shark world

For the true shark fan, it is hard not to have noticed the current craze of 'cage-diving', which only appears to be growing in popularity. This involves being lowered into the water in a 'secure' cage, water which is almost guaranteed to have a good supply of great whites on the prowl.

It has become the latest dare-devil hobby it seems. A bit like bungee jumping, you get the element of fear with the advantage of a 'safety net' protecting you from real harm. Cage-diving with great white sharks has its supporters and critics. One South African diver I know called Karen bought her husband Dave a cage dive as a birthday present. They both absolutely loved it. The thrill of seeing this creature up close and for real yet knowing you were not going to disappear into its tummy is clearly a memory that will stay with them forever.

Others have been scared witless by the experience, with one memorable report in the newspapers showing a great white trying to get to the tourists by shoving his head almost completely inside the top, which is partially open. I don't suppose another go at cage-diving is on that bloke's birthday list.

Since the great whites are lured to the cage with food chucked into the water, there is the argument that great whites will begin to associate the look of divers with dinnertime and that this may increase the likelihood of future attacks on those scubering around minus a cage.

Of course this cannot be proven and there are people (apart from the guys running the cage diving businesses who cannot be expected to give an impartial view), who feel it is a good thing. They say more people being exposed to these creatures and the better understanding they acquire as a result is a benefit to the PR of sharks in general. Personally, image makeover or not, wild horses would not drag me into a cage.

The real victims

While no shark is vegetarian, not all sharks are out to get us. It is a commonly held belief that we cling to, that in the shark/people relationship, it is us who are the victims, yet in reality it is much, much more commonly the other way around.

The more I learn, the more I can see the point of the marine biologists and conservationists. We are at risk of killing off certain species through the various ways that we impose directly on them, from poor fishing practices, in which they get tied up in catches, to our pollution of their environment.

The fishing of sharks for shark-fin soup is one of the most distasteful activities carried out by human beings in regard to sharks. It is staggering that fishermen really do kill sharks simply for their dorsal fins, which are then added to soup in Asia. The shark is often just dumped back in the sea to sink and die. And what makes it worse is that the fin does not even add an amazing flavour or have some culinary property – it is simply in demand because it is rare. Sharks are also caught for the oil they store in their livers and their eyeballs which are used in jewellery-making.

Obviously some sharks are fished for their meat; personally I would not touch this with a barge pole. Sharks, like other large fish such as marlin and albacore tuna, accumulate significant quantities of the man-made toxin methyl mercury which comes from, among other things, the burning of fossil fuels. Methyl mercury is poisonous to our nervous systems and if it builds up, can lead to problems from lack of concentration to severe neurological damage in which your hands begin to curl inwards. The fact that our oceans are so polluted that the fish that live in them are dangerous for us to eat is a spectacular own goal. But in addition it means of course that we are damaging the delicate ecology of marine life from the bottom to the top of the food chain, wrecking everything from corals to sharks as we go.

With declines in some shark populations of 70 per cent being recorded over the past 20–30 years, there is a great urgency for really effective shark conservation and management programmes. If you want to know more about endangered species of sharks, rays and chimaeras, among others, then it is worth logging on to www.redlist.org, which gives the Red List of Threatened Species run by the IUCN, the World Conservation Union. While sharks will inevitably continue to raise a knee-jerk fear in the hearts and minds of many, me included, it is worth pausing for a moment to look at them from the perspective of the coastal people who have lived and fished among them for centuries and who, far from fearing, revere them. A bit of respect can go a long way to keeping both us and them safe and can also prevent an ingrained fear stopping you learn to scuba.

CHAPTER 9

Funny, beautiful and strange:
Nemo and friends

Since the bottom of the pool has a limited attraction, one of the best things about having plucked up the courage to dive in the Indian Ocean was that by the time I had checked my pressure gauge to monitor my air status, kept an eye out for my buddy and gawped at the huge variety of fish, there was less time for my mind to wander off and waste valuable underwater minutes on daft things like my tank going bang or any of the other stuff that I had previously found so scary.

Since it was looking at photographs of the exceptionally beautiful, diverse and extraordinary fish that could be found going about their everyday lives under the water's surface that inspired me to give scuba-diving a try, it is perhaps not surprising that once I came face to face with them, I was totally captivated by what I saw.

As time went by and I felt more comfortable underwater, I found myself dodging home after a dive to do a bit of swotting. Not that it felt like work – it seemed natural to want to know a bit more about the fish and marine life I was diving among. I'm sure this is how most divers feel. Certainly, I've seen some finning around ticking off the fish they have spotted on boards with little fishy pictures on.

Apologies for the seeming lack of imagination by kicking off with Nemo, the small animated clown fish who shot to the world's attention in *Finding Nemo* and who now graces everything from children's flasks and duvet covers to bath mats and shower curtains. But the thing is, clown fish are a great fish to begin with because they have so many unique aspects. The people who made *Finding Nemo* certainly did their research, because these tiny plucky little creatures really do protect their anemones with their lives, feeling no fear, it seems, in coming right up to your mask, giving it a bit of a head butt and even biting your hair to scare you away. To see them in real life is amazing. What I had not appreciated when glued to the cinema screen, watching Nemo's brave dad defending the anemone, was that had it been him who had been gobbled up by a big bad predator, and not Nemo's mum as happened in the story, she could have turned herself into a male fish and taken on the role of guard.

Nor had I realised that no matter how pretty the floating fingers of the anemone may appear when waving in the surge, they carry a deadly sting. Marine biologists have worked out that the clown fish has a mucus covering its body that protects it and allows it to zip in and out of the tentacles without the anemone injuring it. The anemone delivers a nasty sting followed by a chomp to the other fish. By being the only resident in the anemone, the clown fish secures a safe hideout in which to live and breed. All the time it sticks inside, away from fishy predators.

Not all the fish whizzing around look so brightly coloured as the orange and white striped clown fish. This is because water absorbs light very quickly, with the red end of the rainbow's colour spectrum being absorbed first. This means that fish that appear to be blue or a rather dull brown or grey need to have some light shone on them to restore their true beautiful red tones. You can do this easily with a diving torch, and this adds yet more fascination to your diving. The lion fish is a great example. It turns, as if by magic, from an interestingly shaped brown-looking fish into an exotic deep orangey red and white striped one within a moment of your torch catching it.

A very grumpy fish

When diving, you learn very early on not to prod and poke the wildlife underwater. Heaven knows it must be stressful enough for them to have us in their environment without having annoying fingers being pushed at them. With lion fish, there is more reason than with most to follow the rule of looking without touching. While they look all floaty and peaceful, should you make contact with one of their fin spines you will be likely to get a nasty sting. It is simply their form of defence. Lion fish are part of the scorpion fish family and most have venomous spines.

If you thought Victor Meldrew was a grumpy-looking swine, you should take a look at a stone fish – if you can spot them behind their extraordinarily effective, stone-like disguise, that is. Stone fish are in serious need of a dose of happy pills. Ironically, just a quick peek at their deeply disgruntled mouths makes you want to laugh.

If you fancy a giggle, that's fine, but do *not* prod them to see if they will give you a grin back. They won't. Another member of the scorpion fish family, they too have dangerous spines which have actually caused fatalities among humans, even penetrating wetsuits. The pain is supposed to be unbelievably awful, getting gradually worse

over the first 10 minutes after being stung. In some cases, the pain is so extreme that people have fainted – which isn't very good if you are underwater. That information was quite enough to make me keep my hands to myself.

Colour and camouflage

One of my all-time favourites is the parrot fish, presumably thus named because it comes in all the bright colours you would expect to see on its avian namesakes. There are simply loads of different types of parrot fish, from those that are mostly green, to green and purple versions, to others that are orange, green and mauve and some that have a vibrant lovely turquoise colour. The only problem is that parrot fish do not like divers much and tend to dart off as soon as you have spotted them.

The leaf fish is an altogether cooler customer. Another type of scorpion fish, the 'weedy leaf fish' is a variety that could give lessons to the army in the art of camouflage. When I was shown it on a wreck, it took me quite a few minutes to work out where the seaweed ended and the fishy bits began. Only by spotting its eye could you really believe this almost stationary fish, which just swayed gently with the movement of the water, was a fish at all. Once I stayed for 15 minutes, just staring at a leaf fish in total wonder.

You need to apply similar patience if you want to see sand eels. When I was first shown what I can only describe as a 'field' of sand eels, I thought it was just some kind of sea plant waving in the swell like an expanse of growing wheat ready for harvest. But as we swam closer, the 'wheat' disappeared, shooting at high speed back into the bed of sand on the ocean's floor. Only by staying very still for a few minutes did the 'wheat', which, it turned out, was tall, slim, silver-coloured eels, tentatively re-emerge. They poked their heads out, like shy children after a strict telling-off who wondered if it was OK to come back. One movement from me and down, as quick as a flash, they went again, disappearing into their place of protection from predators and nosy scuba-divers.

Having spent ages on one particular dive waiting for the sand eels to pluck up their courage and reappear, I felt a tug on my fin from Gérald. I was bit cross really, since he blew my cover and they retreated at lightning speed. But I soon forgot all of that as I turned to see the most beautiful ray glide over my head. As it gracefully passed by it left a tremendous sense of peace in its wake, although it was hard not to notice its sting, a rather lethal-looking hook on its tail which, on a bit of further reading, turned out to be an particularly venomous barb. Another case of Look Don't Touch.

One ray that I've never had the fortune to see is the manta ray. Tony, a diver I met recently who has had the immense pleasure of diving with them in the Maldives, says they are absolutely gigantic, often reaching a good 3 metres across. When I saw a video taken of him swimming with these massive sea creatures, I felt like I was watching *Star Wars*, as three or four swam towards the camera and whooshed overhead.

Yet while immense in proportions, manta rays offer no problem to divers. It's the days of the surrounding plankton that are numbered as these ancient fish, which are related distantly to sharks, cruise by. Their big horns, which resemble a catamaran and look rather ferocious, are there simply to steer the plankton into its ever-hungry mouth.

A quick freshen-up

Although I have banged on about not ever probing or touching the local fish and marine life, in some cases, an experienced dive leader may handle the locals if he is very familiar with them. I was surprised to see a diver once remove his regulator and allow a couple of shrimps to hop inside his mouth. Crikey! Was he about to have an underwater meal I thought? A lunch of raw shrimps? No, it seemed not. It turned out these were little cleaner prawns, happy to have a quick nosh on debris in his teeth. When we were encouraged to let them hop onto our hands to have a little wash and brush up, to my surprise they did not feel as though they were biting or giving me a quick nip, but they left a ticklish sensation, like a duster brushing over my skin. I've never seen any of the instructors offer their open mouth to another crustacean: the lobster. With their rather large pincers snapping for dear life in front of them, it is not surprising. They look as though they would whip your teeth out minus anaesthetic, like an old-fashioned dentist, rather than act like a toothbrush.

Identifying new friends

Often, when I've surfaced from a dive, I'll hear people say, 'Wow, did you see the —?' while I'm thinking 'Gosh, what a lovely yellow fish I just saw.' The long Latin names can be a bit too much to remember, but the common names are easy to pick up and often make complete sense, describing the fish perfectly.

The butterfly fish is a good example. Also known as the banner fish, both names do a good job of describing it. There are lots of species, but some, which are black and white striped with a yellow tail and fin, have a long fin that seems to come out of its first black stripe and wave around like a long, thin banner as it swims. While butterfly fish are pretty easy to recognise, others may not be so obvious. Sometimes even the locals get confused, especially since some reef fish change their shape, size and even colour as they grow from juveniles into fully fledged adult fish.

A diver friend in Mauritius told me that he once came across a tiny reef fish on a dive that he had never seen before. The following day he returned to the same spot and, on locating it again, excitedly took its photograph, which he duly emailed to an expert he knew in Germany. The reply was rapid and succinct: it was just a baby version of an extremely common reef fish that he saw on virtually every one of his dives. Sure enough, he looked it up and there it was: one of his daily regulars with which he was so familiar.

Growing up

It is fascinating to see the young versions of fish gradually alter with age. I love one particular little fish called the yellow box fish. There are one or two at a dive site that I have been to often, floating around with a pompous look on their flat faces, which look a bit like those of boxer dogs. When young, the tiny yellow box fish is not much bigger than half of your thumb and is bright yellow with black polka dots, bobbing around like someone inflated it with a bicycle pump. One of the reasons why box fish look so odd is because unlike most fish which have, like us, skeletons made of bone on the inside, the skeleton of the box fish is made from plates of bone on top of which is their skin and inside of which is their organs – they live inside a bony box like brightly wrapped-up Christmas gifts. Because they have only tiny little fins to propel them, they do have a touch of the preposterous about them, even more because of their plump, Angelina Jolie, 'kiss me quick' lips. But back to the point, which is that as yellow box fish grow up, their bright yellow colour dulls down to a more golden hue, and the little black dots divide into a repeating pattern all over their body of three black and one white dot. And as it gets bigger it slims down, like it's been slightly deflated, taking on an altogether more fish-like and less puffed-up appearance.

Talking of puffed-up fish, there is a family known as puffer fish, and one puffer fish in particular tends to sits on the ocean floor at the Cathedral dive site in Flic en Flac. This is another exception to the rule when it comes to touching. The instructors and dive master in charge 'know' this particular puffer fish and know that it rather enjoys a gentle stroke on its back by a careful diver. Its surface feels like velvet to touch, it is so soft and silky, and the puffer fish is happy to loll around waiting for a bit of human affection.

I have met other divers in Mauritius who have developed a great affinity with moray eels. These can be absolutely enormous and, frankly, I'm more than happy to see them with just their heads popping out of the holes in which they live. With their jaws opening and closing rhythmically to catch passing food, this is quite close enough for me. Yet some will come out when they detect the presence of a diver they know and trust and can be handled like a snake, curling their sometimes 3-metre bodies gently around the torso, arms and legs of the diver, and responding to a stroke like a cat, stretching themselves out. You can almost hear them purring. Even so, when I've watched this lovely relationship in action, I've kept my eyes fixed on the mouth of the Moray, making sure it is not about to have a funny turn and come bombing after me.

Tights and teeth

Another fascinating creature is the octopus, whose eyes seem to be almost hidden behind heavy lids for most of the time, but when open, are intensely black and piercing. As for their legs, well I have to admit, as I discovered on a trip to Rodrigues, they are delicious in curry. There, a speciality is dried octopus. The women catch them and then hang them on their washing lines like eight-legged pairs of American Tan tights. As tasty as they are, octopuses are much nicer when you see them going about their daily business. Personally, once they have locked their beady eyes on me, I feel as though I am quite close enough. Since, not surprisingly, they don't like human contact much, again it is best to steer clear. Why go looking for trouble when it has been known for octopuses to give divers a bite (and to sit on their heads, remember the legs-around-the-diver's-neck story?). As well as their bites being flipping painful, I am told that some of them have venom in their saliva which can do extra damage.

But as ever, exceptions to the rule do exist. My friend Anja was diving in the Maldives once with an instructor who had got to know a local octopus who bobbed out of its cave to say 'Hi' when she passed. One day, she used her new, brightly coloured red diving knife to point in its direction. It seems that it took an immediate fancy to the knife, probably attracted by the bright colour. It deftly whipped the knife from her hand and shot back into its cave, apparently happy with its new home decoration because the knife has never been spat back out.

Fish that do spit things out are the titan trigger fish. These are, in my view, proper 'fish'-looking fish, the kind you drew as a kid with plump, oval bodies and yellowish blue colours with groovy turquoise fins. I've spent ages watching them hoovering up what I thought were bits of rocks and then regurgitating them. I thought that maybe they were sharpening their teeth, but it seems this is not the case. What they are actually doing is eating coral. They eat the algae bit inside and then, quite sensibly, spit out the remaining hard bit that they don't want. You find them doing this in the Indian Ocean and the Red Sea and, although you are quite safe looking on, if they are guarding their nests on the ocean bed, then take care. Those gnashers, which are sharp enough to bite into coral, can do divers real damage, not surprisingly, and if you go near them when they are carrying out nest-watching duties, they can charge you at a hefty old speed. If you are lucky, they will simply ram you. If less fortunate, they may sink those sharp incisors into your wetsuit and possibly your flesh. Not nice.

Another fish with sharp fangs is the barracuda. I thought that Thierry, the owner of Sun Divers, was having a serious laugh when, having spotted a school of barracuda circling under the boat post-dive, he suggested getting in and swimming with them. Everyone had a go and although I was rather cowardly, when I saw that everyone was still in one piece, I eventually joined them. One barracuda alone is, I am told, much more dangerous than a big shoal, which was just as well, because these long slim fish with razor-sharp teeth and 'go faster' stripes on their bodies were soon surrounding us and circling like crazy. There we were, in the middle of the shoal as they whizzed round and round. It was amazing and actually too extraordinary for me to feel worried. If you do not provoke them, barracuda should leave you alone, mostly because they actually like to eat things like squid and reef fish, not chunks of people in wetsuits.

Snooty gents and spaghetti

I find that long, thin fish do tend to look a bit mean, although that cannot be said for the harmless funny-looking trumpet fish that I bumped into on one of my first times underwater. My first encounter with this long, day-glo yellow fish made me want to reach for the sunglasses, it was so brightly coloured. I could not help thinking that, with the brown markings on its head that looked from a distance like a pair of haughty nostrils, it resembled Kenneth Williams. I felt quite sure that it would start saying 'Oh Matron!' at any moment. At its other end, the tail had markings that made it look like a head, presumably to fox its predators, giving it a 'push-me, pull-me' look.

Although the trumpet fish looks quite amusing, it has a crafty line of attack when it comes to its own hunting methods, which involve sneaking up on small fish by swimming alongside another fish which keeps it hidden from view. Then … Bang! It comes flying out, all guns blazing or, in this case, mouth open as wide as its whole body, as it sucks in the unsuspecting prey. But Nature is a dog-eat-dog world, and in their turn, a trumpet fish can make a tasty meal for a lion fish. Gérald has a photo of the latter which, having hovered silently above a trumpet fish for ages, suddenly launched its attack and swallowed the fish whole, leaving, as his photo shows, just its tail hanging out. The lion fish looks like a child frantically sucking in a piece of spaghetti.

After one dive, I was bobbing around on the surface, chatting to the others while we waited for the boat to pick us up. 'Ah, did you see that fish carrying a baby in its mouth, just like a kangaroo in its mother's pouch?' I said. Everyone turned and stared as if I was a total simpleton. Clearly I was being one. 'It was eating it, you wally!' came the unilateral response. I felt awful, realising that the fish had been swallowed tail first and that I'd witnessed its last moments, eyes still blinking and still very much alive as it was consumed in slow motion.

I had a much gentler experience, away from such underwater battle zones of life and death when I was fortunate enough to spot a turtle, or, rather, when Gérald spotted it for me. What surprised me most was how very timid these big and lumbering animals are. Almost as soon as you have spotted them, they will turn tail and, at a quite unlumbering speed, zip off in the other direction, demonstrating that when they are worried, they are extremely agile and do not dawdle at all. With a particularly keen-eyed skipper like Soonan, however, I have been lucky enough to see some turtles at the surface when they come up for air. They do not stay for long, but it is a thrill to catch a glimpse. The same is true of catching sight of a dolphin's dorsal fin. Seeing these beautiful creatures rolling through the waves is mesmerising. Safely watching from a boat is as close as I have ever wanted to get. While other divers revel in swimming among the dolphins, their sheer power is awe-inspiring enough for me to observe from a distance.

Fascinating slugs

While the bigger creatures of the sea are spectacular, personally, I find myself getting completely engrossed by the smaller life. One marine animal in particular that I just love to spot is the sea slug. OK, it may not sound very pretty, let's be honest – its greyish brown land-living counterpart is hardly anything to get excited about. However, underwater sea slugs, more correctly known as 'nudibranchs' have been bestowed with intricate patterns and colours that make them appear like jewels. Often just half a finger in length, they are not that easy to spot unless you move quite slowly, but when you do find one, it is hard not to be impressed by their Technicolor dreamcoats.

I was surprised to find out that these largely inanimate-looking creatures were carnivores. You can't see them while on a dive, but they have a surprisingly strong set of jaws made from chitin, the same hard substance found in the shells of crabs and prawns, and they have tiny little teeth which allow them to munch on soft corals, anemones and sometimes sponges. Like land slugs, nudibranchs (the name means 'naked gills' because their gills are on the outside surrounding their bottoms), move around at a snail's pace on one 'foot', which stretches all the way along its underside and which oozes mucus that helps it to get a good grip on the rock.

Some, although I've not often seen them, live on the sand, and they have little hairs poking down from their foot which help them to move smoothly over the mucus. What with gills on their bottoms and mucus-exuding feet, I suppose I wasn't that surprised to discover that when it comes to reproducing, their essential organs are on their necks. I'm told they position themselves next to each other facing, rather anti-socially, in opposite directions. This is not because they don't like the look of each other but to efficiently pass little sacs of sperm between themselves, a bit like exchanging precious birthday gifts.

Anyway, reproduction aside, once you have seen a nudibranch, resplendent in its colourful robes, it makes you feel sorry for its dull, terrestrial relatives. One particular version that I just had to look up (if I'm being a nudibranch nerd, skip this bit) is called *Chromodoris geminus*. I remember the name, because it reminds me of a waitress called Doris who used to work in my granddad's restaurant and who wore an apron with a similar pattern to that found on this particular nudibranch. It is essentially a lovely daffodil-yellow colour with white blobs, inside of which are purple dots. On its frilly edges there is a slim band of pale grey followed by a band of white. On its back part, it has about 11 little white tufts with grey edges which, although they are its gills, look like a sprout of rather wild hair. At the other end it has two little yellow-tipped 'horns'. To me it is, and always will be, the 'Doris's Apron' nudibranch. Another one looks like Coco the Clown. It has a milky, translucent white body that looks a bit like cooked squid, with a colourful yellow edge and six big red polka dots. It is hard to imagine that it survives mostly by noshing on sponges, but that's its favourite food, so there we are.

Electric-shocked porcupines

I promise not to drone on about any more after these last two, but you have to see these tiny works of art to believe them; they leave Fabergé eggs standing. One, *Phyllidia varicose* ('Phyllis's varicose veins' to you and me, and don't ask me where that name comes from, I've no idea but it helps when I'm trying to recall the Latin stuff) is black, but has three white ridges running lengthways along its body. These ridges are topped with yellow knobs. Like a lot of nudibranchs (and fortunately for me since this is where I mostly have been diving), they are found throughout the waters of the Indian Ocean. Finally, there is the *Cuthona* genus, which is bright pinky mauve in colour and topped with long cerata tipped with yellow. It looks like a multicoloured porcupine that has had an electric shock. It really is hard to take your eyes off these marvellous creations.

I could go on and on. The oceans are jam packed with the beautiful and the extraordinary. The only sad thing is that with all the pollution we create in this world and with the environmentally unfriendly way in which a lot of fishing is still carried out, how much longer they will remain here for us to enjoy is not known. It is a troubling question which needs to be addressed rapidly.

Making your mind up

Where you choose to dive in the world certainly dictates what you are likely to see when it comes to fish. The most important thing is to do your homework and be aware that all is not necessarily as the travel agent may tell you. Not that it is their fault or that they are misleading you deliberately. Things move quickly in the marine world and areas that were once well known for certain life may have changed when you come to book.

Nothing is more frustrating than to see divers rock up at a dive centre with looks of huge anticipation on their face, saying, 'Hey, take me to the manta rays' when none have been spotted in local waters for a good 10 years. It is a come-down for them and immediately makes the dive centre feel as though they will not be coming up with the expected goods. It is therefore well worth getting on the phone to the dive centre while still at home, to ask them directly what you are likely to see if you pay them a visit. Many now have websites which will fully describe the local fishy inhabitants as well.

While Mauritius, for example, is great for gorgeous reef fish and nudibranches, if it is a whole load of mantas you are after then go to the Maldives. If it is whale sharks you are seeking, then head to Mozambique or Western Australia. Should you wish to guarantee scubering among hammerhead sharks, then you should head to Columbia to dive off the island of Malpelo; the place is teaming with these extraordinary looking beasts.

Some people I know yearn for nothing more than to dive under the ice in frozen lakes and seas. Should you wish to give this a go in, for instance, a frozen lake in Austria, you probably won't see much more than a very hardy perch or two.

These days you can dive everywhere from the Black Sea to the massively popular, and much more familiar, Red Sea. While the former offers crystal clear waters once you have swum through lots of jellyfish, the latter is known for its plethora of beautiful fish along with the amazing, prehistoric looking dugongs. These kind of resemble a hippopotamus, but with a massive fishtail at the back and a snout which makes it look like one of those industrial cleaners you see staff manfully handling to clean the concourses at railway stations. You can also spot them in both Northern and Western Australia apparently, while its close relative the manatee hangs out in the waters off the Florida coast.

You can dive in Thailand and Tahiti, in Cuba and the Comores, the Seychelles and Singapore. And of course, closer to home, you can plop into the waters in European dive destinations, including the coast of England. Here, if you are lucky enough, you can see seals off the coast of Cornwall, and who knows, maybe a basking shark near Bognor!

CHAPTER 10

The wonders of a night dive: Phosphorescent plankton, day-glo squid and pegged-out parrot fish

At first, when Gérald suggested that I come on a 'night' dive, I thought he'd finally lost his marbles. It was one thing to dive in the crystal clear sea, where you can see for miles around. I thought that, frankly, I'd done pretty well getting to the stage where I could enjoy the experience. But every time you get comfy-ish with scuba-diving, it seems that there is another challenge lurking just around the corner. And plunging into an inky black sea, which for me immediately conjured images of giant octopus legs lying just below the surface waiting to grab you and drag you down into oblivion was, it seemed, the next 'experience'.

Being with divers who have been there, seen it, done it can sometimes be a confidence drainer, but there was something comforting about leaving the shore onboard a boat with a gang of six, all of whom had done such dives before and had not only lived to tell the tale, but simply couldn't wait to be back in the moonlit briny.

As we chugged away from the beach just before sunset, with Soonan at the helm, I have to admit that the nerves in my stomach were calmed by the serenity of the moment. It was truly beautiful to see the sun gradually slipping away from the day while out at sea rather than just watching it from the shore. That said, the moment that it finally dipped beyond my view, the butterflies began to rise. And yet even so, there was a peace about the evening and a quietness that seemed to take away just some of the fear of back-rolling into the darkness. Once again, faith in my instructor was the key for my even agreeing to set foot in the boat for this dive. And faith, I might add, in our skipper Soonan. It always amazes me how he and the instructors find the exact position of the dive sites during the day time; to manage it at night shows that they truly know their navigating. Maybe, as I always imagine dolphins to have, they possess an inbuilt global positioning system lurking in their brains.

Having arrived at the right spot, I paid 100 per cent attention to the briefing and was clutching my torch as if it were my lifeline, which, once you are underwater, it pretty much is. You don't just need it to see where you are going and to enable you, your buddy and your diving group to stick together, but you also need it to read your pressure gauge to see how much air you have left. I was happy to see that when I shone my torch on my gauge it became illuminated, like a watch I remember my brother once getting for Christmas back in the days of chopper bikes and shoes with a mini compass in the heel. I noticed that some people had a back-up torch as well which, given that torches, like most things in life, are fallible and can go wrong, is also well worth having.

I was extremely pleased to be diving on a site that I had been to quite a few times during the day, so I knew its layout fairly well. Knowing the site makes a lot of sense when doing a night dive, for obvious reasons. The conditions were excellent. This is essential, I discovered, as our dive was postponed a few times because the sea had been too rough. No diving centre worth its salt will take you out if there is a problem with a rough sea, if the visibility is poor or if currents have picked up. With all my confidence boosters in place, I still felt that sitting on the edge of the boat about to back-roll into the darkness below seemed like total insanity. It was only seeing and hearing the others sploshing overboard that gave me the courage to go. There was no luxury in loitering on a night dive, it was now or never. Splash!

Follow the bubbles

One of the things I wondered about before the night dive was how would I know which way up I was? Once I had back-rolled and was holding onto the anchor line, it was easy because I was still quite close to the surface. But how, I was musing, would I know once down on the dive for real? Needless to say, this kind of question was covered in the pre-dive briefing. Gérald explained that you simply look at which way your bubbles are going as you breathe. You are the right way up when your bubbles are going up! When underwater it was easy to see how this worked.

Is it disorientating? Yes. Can you see much? Not to start with. Does it get better? Yes. Once I had found my way to the anchor line and was both the right way up and still breathing, lo and behold, I began to see! It's like when you turn out the lights or go outside in the dark: your eyes make 'visual purple', a pigment in the retina of your eyes that helps your eyesight to adapt and to make out things in the darkness. It is no different underwater. Gradually things become clearer. I couldn't see far, but it was no longer pitch black.

As we gradually went down on the anchor line, the moment of letting go and diving in the dark for real arrived. I'm not sure that I moved more than 3 centimetres from Gérald's side for the first 10 minutes of the dive. I may as well have been attached to his fins, so closely did I follow the buddy principle of sticking together. As the time moved on I realised that the other divers were an incredibly sensible lot and were all staying in a tightish group, so I tried to ease myself away ... just a little.

The sights I saw that night will stay with me for life. Good grief. Forget Disneyland. Forget sci-fi movies. The stuff that goes on in our oceans, even within the first 20 metres of the surface, is out of this world. Just as on land, while some animals, like domestic dogs, tend to sleep at nightfall, tomcats are out there prowling the streets, living the nocturnal high life. Similarly, fish and marine life that normally stay out of sight during the daytime are up and about the moment the sun goes down.

Plankton light display

If I had to pick one thing out of my night-diving experiences that impressed me most it would have to be the plankton. During daytime dives you don't really see it. It's just there in the water floating around, unseen and, from my point of view, not given a moment's thought, which is a bit bad really, because when you get down to it, life itself depends on plankton, since the 6 billion tonnes that grow in our oceans each year pumps out almost half of the oxygen produced in our world. Plankton comes in two main forms, phyto (plant) plankton and zoo (animal) plankton. The smallest plant planktons are cyanobacteria, which are just one cell in size, with green and blue pigments, but it is the dinoflagellates that are a gift from heaven to the night diver.

It's as though the dinoflagellates get dressed up for a night on the tiles. We had been briefed that at one point on our dive we would all kneel on the seabed in a circle and switch off our torches because, when you do this and then move your arms around, you disturb the plankton, which are bioluminant – in other words they are able to create light in their own bodies. This means that the plankton lights up like microscopic sparks, as though someone had scattered stardust all around. It's breathtaking, it's like watching the stars at night but actually being surrounded by them. They seem to move with your hands and fins. It's such a special ambiance down there. As you swoosh your arms around you feel like you're holding hundreds of sparklers on November 5th. Then, as a diver swims off in front of you, they leave a trail of phosphorescence in their ghostly wake. When back on land it is hard to imagine that it happened at all.

Light for life

It's not only plankton that has the power to glow in the dark. Some fish do so too, even at the shallow depths of recreational night dives. However, when you go way, way down in special submersibles to depths of 150 metres and more, where it is dark all the time and where there is no distinction between day or night, many more creatures create light for a range of functions, from protection and camouflage to hunting. Light, in underwater life, is made in one of two ways. One is by burning a substance called luciferin in the presence of the enzyme luciferase. We have loads of enzymes in our bodies, whizzing around doing everything from breaking down the proteins we eat (proteases) to the sugar in milk (lactase) and even alcohol (alcohol dehydrogenase). Similarly, some marine plant plankton have luciferin and luciferase to do the job of lighting themselves up. The second way is from bacteria which, incredibly enough, grow their own light organs and live inside fish. Eat your heart out the National Grid. While we need the likes of fossil fuels and nuclear power to generate electrical light, these squillions-of-years-old marine dwellers have light-making enzymes and are their very own internal generators.

Hot on the tail of the phosphorescent plankton came the other wonders that the dark ocean waters revealed as we sought out the nightlife with our torches. The lobsters were spectacular in their colourful suits. I had no idea just how many colours a lobster has. Having seen them cooked on a plate I imagined that they are a pinkish red, full stop. How wrong was I? Very, it seems. As they good-naturedly allowed us to take a peek into their night-time lifestyles, the purples, greens, pinks and crimsons flashed back at us and their eyes, which stared right at us like head lamps, cut through the darkness.

And then there were the squid. Again, philistine that I am, a squid to me was the translucent white seafood which tastes great when pan fried with garlic and herbs. See it underwater at night and it puts on a show like the Cirque du Soleil. The squid we saw had large turquoise bands surrounding its eyes and a glowing pink body through which you could clearly see its intestines as it whizzed by, changing colours as it went. As Gérald shone his light on one fly-past, it pulled up its legs above its head in defence, like Frank

Bruno about to launch a quick right hook, ducking and diving as it went.

As we swung around to follow its movements, Gérald spotted his favourite night creature, the Spanish dancer. Exotically named after the flamboyant flamenco dancers, it

is in fact a type of nudibranch, in other words a sea slug, although you would never have guessed so. The biggest of the bunch, Gérald had told me pre-dive that we would be really blessed if we got to see one and that if we did, when he shone his torch on it, it would lift its 'wings' and dance in the light. It was true. These frilly, beautiful nudibranchs, which come in shades of pink and red and orange, put on a performance that the Royal Ballet would be proud of.

An old favourite

As if this had not been enough of a treat, there was more to come, in the form of a certain type of parrot fish. Quite how my regulator stayed in my mouth is still a mystery to me, as my jaw practically dropped open when I saw the slumbering version of one of my elusive day-dive favourites. There it was, resting, utterly peacefully and, for once, still and thus possible to study at close range. What was even more amazing was that it was lying within what looked like a soft, transparent, jelly-like sleeping bag. Because you can't chat underwater I could only stare in astonishment. The questions would have to come after we'd surfaced. Had I not been nudged on by the divers following up from behind, I think I'd still be there now staring at this extraordinary sight. As soon as my head was out of the water, I was spluttering out my need for answers.

It seems that some types of parrot fish, usually the smaller ones who are less physically able to beat off predators, make these protective bags to sleep in. They produce the bag from their own saliva and it helps to protect them from becoming a tasty meal to a large fish out on a night hunt, because other fish can't smell them through their sac. I suppose the next question was inevitable. How on earth do they get themselves out of these bags once they wake in the morning?

My question would only be answered a year later, when I set off on a night/dawn dive off Rodrigues, with Benoit, of Bouba Diving Centre. The dive is not for those who like their sleep because you have to be down at the boat, kitted up and ready to go, at 5am. The idea is that you start your dive in the dark, experience the sun coming up while underwater and finish it as a day dive. It is a fantastic experience for many reasons, not least because I found the answer to the parrot-fish question, which is that it eats its way out of its cocoon. Incredible. It gobbles it up as if it were a tasty breakfast of pain au chocolat and off it goes, zooming about its daily chores and still very much in one piece, having survived the risk of becoming a night-time morsel.

This whole night dive in reverse is certainly worth doing. Just as we saw nocturnal fish come to life when diving at sundown, so they were winding down as the dawn was breaking. The experience of watching the sun rise when diving, as the turtles in *Finding Nemo* would say 'really rocks'.

And as for night-diving, after my first trip, when we were all out of the water and safely ensconced back on the boat, a friend Tony from Yorkshire summed up the experience. 'That,' he said 'was the dog's b*****ks.' It was hard to translate into French for Gérald and Italian for the other divers, but from the beaming smiles that accompanied Tony's enthusiastic declaration, I think that they got his drift.

Thrill-seekers

For all the thrills and spills of night-diving, my experience has only been on the safest of sites where it is unlikely that anything large or scary would come flying out of the blue or, in this case, out of the black. This is more than can be said for my friend Anya's experiences in the Maldives, when sharks suddenly appeared from nowhere. No one appeared to be worried, and she is one of those incorrigible thrill-seekers, so for her, it was the best possible outcome because the sharks were harmless and she loves a bit of action.

Which is probably why she also loved the idea of night-diving in Bodensee, a lake in Germany, on a dive site called the Devil's Desk. That sounded even more alarming than the sharks. Along with the usual healthy adrenaline flow that goes with a night dive, came tales of unpredictable currents having suddenly sucked divers down onto the lake's deep dark bottom many metres down. I got goose bumps just hearing about this dive, where everyone was attached to a rope for safety. Not for me the likes of the Devil's Desk, although this dive is actually no longer allowed.

Nor do I think I'd much fancy the experience of jumping out of a helicopter, fully kitted up, and plunging into a dark Austrian lake in the mountains at 2,000 metres up. This was a night dive that required a lot of preparation, said Anya, who regaled me with the details. Her training included jumping into a pool from the diving board with all her scuba gear on, as well as plenty of mental preparation to help cope with the inevitable fears sparked by actually doing it for real.

Personally, I'd rather stick to the safe stuff, to dives with which I am familiar, with people I know, feel at ease with and have confidence in. Since preparation is so important when diving, wherever and whenever you happen to be going, there is one more thing I should mention regarding night-diving: spare a moment's thought for a hot flask of tea or hot chocolate and some biscuits to share on the boat ride back. Not to mention plenty of warm towels. You won't have the sun to give you a post-dive toasting on the way back to the dive centre.

The provisions came in especially handy one night when some wag had decided to remove our big white bucket from the marker indicating the pass back through the reef (the point where the reef is deep enough so a boat can pass above it). With us all yelling different and unhelpful directions to Soonan in several different languages, we bobbed around for an hour trying to locate the way through. It was a classic case of everyone thinking they could manage the England squad better than Sven (or whichever poor blighter happens at the time to be lumbered with that poisoned chalice). Quite why Soonan didn't just flip us all overboard and tell us to swim I'll never know.

All I can say is that it is a good job that diving burns up lots of calories. As many, apparently, as playing an energetic game of squash. You burn them up mostly because your body has to heat the air in your tank – which is the temperature of the water around you – to body temperature. And you also burn off extra calories keeping the rest of your body warm. Just as well, given the number of biscuits we got through while bobbing around in search of the bucketless pole.

But we didn't just have biscuits and dive stories to entertain us. The Pearl Beach Hotel, just in front of the pass, was having a knees-up that night, so we were kept amused by silhouettes of people dancing in the nightclub lights, although they were not a patch on the twinkling plankton and Spanish dancers we had seen beneath the sea.

Eventually, when their disco lights got brighter, Soonan's patience, as always, paid off and the position of the pass came into view. Through we whizzed, back to bask in the memories of that wonderful underwater night time world.

CHAPTER 11

Diving bores and know-it-alls

Recently, Gérald was together with some of his instructor friends and they were regaling us with stories. One of them was telling us how a slight problem with a language barrier made him realise that he needed to refine his diver briefings. This happened during one particular dive, after he had described to some beginners the kind of finning motion that you should make with your legs when scuba diving. In order to be sure they understood, he demonstrated what he meant by using his arms. He put them straight out in front of him and replicated the movement that they should make with their legs, up and down in a scissor action.

Once underwater he glanced over to check his diver, only to see him moving his arms up and down in front of him, both as straight as a die, and looking a bit like Frankenstein, exactly as he had done on the boat. The diver had clearly got the wrong end of the stick and thought you did this movement with your arms *and* your legs. As my friend looked down, he saw another diver doing precisely the same with a dive master friend looking on in astonishment at this new scubering style.

While scuba-diving can often provide amusing anecdotes, not all tales are as interesting to the non-diver and I'm sure that most divers hooked on the sport are capable of boring the socks off friends and family over their underwater exploits. Hands up, I know that I am guilty of the crime but, like most divers, I quickly learnt to read the glazed looks of feigned interest and move, albeit unwillingly, onto more universally accepted topics of conversation. Some divers, however, just don't seem to get it and go on about their sub-aquatic exploits in a way that even the most enthusiastic fan can find tedious. From what my non-diving friends have said, it seems there is nothing worse than having a crushing diving bore yap in your ear for hours on end about how you *must* give it a go. If you are teetering on the edge of the 'to dive or not to dive' decision and run into one of these, try touching them gently on the arm and saying something along the lines of, 'You've absolutely convinced me that I really must give taking up diving some serious thought.' It sounds convincing but is totally non-committal. Then rapidly change the subject.

Dyed-in-the-wool diving nuts talking about their passion are, in the main, a harmless breed. They are just fanatical about diving, 'fans' in the truest sense of the word. Personally, I can listen to them for hours.

Know-it-alls, on the other hand, can be quite a different matter, and I try to avoid them at all costs, especially as a buddy. I have found that they are not too hard to spot, often giving themselves away on sight by arriving at the dive centre with every gadget known to the diving-equipment world dangling from their brand spanking new, tailor-made Prada-designed wetsuit. In even the briefest of conversations, they tend to live up to my initial assessment by launching immediately into not just how competent *they* are, but also giving you plenty of tips and advice on how *you* should be diving as well.

All the gear

Staggering to the boat under the weight of their wide variety of big impressive dive knives strapped to their calves, torches the size of spot lights, spare navigational compasses and nets, these walking Christmas trees of the recreational diving world were, for me, a little unnerving when I was just starting out. My reaction on first seeing one such diver board the boat was to take a look at my

own gear and think, 'Crikey, does he know something I don't? Has the dive centre underestimated the conditions of this dive?'

I remember feeling very small next to one particular chap who arrived to dive at a centre fully kitted out in brand-new gear. It turned out that he had not taken so much as a single breath underwater. Worse still, it looked as though he never would. Having ticked the 'I have asthma' box on the centre's medical form, diving was simply not an option for him. Maybe he sold his kit on eBay. I felt very sorry for him, but it is worth checking that you are fit to dive and perhaps giving it a go with gear borrowed from the centre where you learn, rather than plunging in and wasting a fortune.

I recall another diver who had, in addition to the standard gear, and this is the honest truth, two extra dive computers, two knives, one on each leg, three pencils, two boards to write on (one in his BCD pocket, the other on his arm), a 2-metre hose for his alternate air source, an AIR2 (which is an extra direct source of air) in his BCD and two surface parachutes (which you inflate on coming up so the dive boat can spot you). Finally, he was sporting a special 'black box' contraption which, if he pressed a button, would send a signal via satellite to a global monitoring service that would precisely pinpoint his location and launch a rescue.

I was quivering by the time I'd clocked all this gear. There are, no doubt, plenty of occasions when this type of equipment may be eminently sensible to have about your person. In certain demanding situations, it might be absolutely essential. However, it was, I discovered on discreetly checking with our instructor, slightly over the top for a five-person sortie that, as well as being led by an instructor, had an accompanying dive master to boot and was in clear waters on a calm day.

We all back-rolled and down we went. All seemed to be going smoothly until, as we were ascending, I glimpsed, out of the side of my mask, a bit of a commotion going on to my left. As I looked around, it seemed that the over-laden diver had been so busy checking all his gadgets that he was not aware he had neglected a basic aspect of diving safety: his buddy's air supply. His buddy was fast running out and, in the end, his 2-metre alternative air source hosing did come in handy but for very unnecessary reasons. Had he not had so much gear to keep monitoring, his buddy probably wouldn't have got into trouble in the first place. He would have realised they needed to end their dive earlier.

False sense of security

I have come to realise that there is no point being intimidated by people rocking up and going on about their latest, high-tech, expensive gear 'that you really *must* get'. If you know that your gear is in good working order and is suitable for the dive you are doing, I think that it is best to put their views out of your mind. Despite being fully qualified, some of these over-equipped, over-the-top Liberaces of the diving world are not the best people to take advice from. I have learnt not to be lulled into a false sense of security by those with long lists of qualifications and egos more inflated than their BCDs. However much confidence they appear to have, I find that it is always better to listen to and follow the advice of the local diver who knows the dive sites and the local conditions.

Accidents can happen if you don't heed this advice, as one diver from the Seychelles explained to me: 'I was on a dive once where the others who were on our boat clearly thought they knew more than the local dive master. Big mistake: the best divers are the ones who are in charge and dive there all the time. I've been in several situations where I have done my pre-dive brief, explaining exactly where we are going and how long for, and as soon as these types enter the water, off they go on their own sweet way, thinking they know better.

'On one such occasion, we were on a dive which I knew, given the conditions of the day, would have quite a bit of current at the end. I told them to stick close to the drop-off to get protection from this current as we were ascending, but did they listen? No. They ignored my dive plan and went away from the protective wall. Quite literally, within 3 seconds, whoosh, they were gone.'

Their action had several ramifications. The others in the group who witnessed the event themselves started to stress, which put them at risk of an uncontrolled ascent, while the missing divers themselves were nowhere to be seen when the main group surfaced. Despite alerting local fisherman and conducting their own search of the sea, the two divers remained lost to the group for 3 hours. 'Just as we were giving up and heading back home, I spotted two heads bobbing around. Boy, were they sorry they hadn't listened.' As Gérald says, it is vital to always remember that however good your equipment and however many dives you've done and however much experience you have, compressed air is compressed air and diving is diving. Safety comes first every time.

Local know-how

Not listening to out-of-town know-it-alls is, in my view, a step in the right direction when putting this rule into practice. Not following their lead underwater does not just involve sticking with the group rather than being persuaded by some over-confident nutcase to go roaring off and breaking the dive plan as if you were Bonnie and Clyde, it also means not being tempted to touch the wildlife, even if they break the rules and do so. Teasing a moray eel isn't funny or clever, it can get you bitten. In addition, you should never follow a know-it-all into caves or wrecks if you have been briefed not to. There will always be a good reason for local rules, which are there for your own safety.

I always remember asking my uncle who was a pilot how on earth he coped with the stress of having so many passengers' lives in his hands. 'I don't think about them,' he said in all honesty. 'It's getting myself down safely that I care about!' It may sound hugely selfish but it is the best response you could actually hope for when you think about it and the same, I think, goes for instructors and dive masters. The ones to trust are the ones that take their own safety really seriously. They want to get through the dive with everyone intact. Any underwater dramas with their divers put them in danger too and that is the last thing they want!

I have also discovered that it is most unwise to get sucked into the obsession some divers have with depth. They appear to be driven by an unseen force to notch up a deeper and deeper figure on their computer. I have often found myself deliberately backing away, not wanting to get hyped up by their big talk out of the water or to be coaxed into trying something my local dive expert doesn't recommend.

I have also learnt to resist feeling pressured by these big talkers into doing a dive that either I simply don't feel like doing on a particular day, or I am not up to in terms of experience. As my course taught me, sometimes it is easier to just say that you have a problem equalising your ears, which every diver respects, than trying to explain to an over-bearing diver the real reasons behind your decision not to take part in the dive. No professional diving outfit is going to get upset by your being honest with them, but some individual divers just don't get it so, as I've found in some cases, it is simply not worth trying.

Family arguments

I was chit-chatting with Gérald one day about this, and he mentioned that sometimes the person putting you under pressure is known to you, a relative for instance, and this can be much trickier. He says it is quite common and he tries delicately to intervene. On one occasion he actually ended up telling a father to back off and returned his fee because he was yelling loudly at a sobbing 13-year-old to get on with the dive and not to waste his money. 'It was clear that the child was terrified but the father wasn't listening.' Hard to fathom but it can happen. In another case, a child had bad asthma, an absolute out-and-out reason never to dive, and yet the mother was still insisting they should have a go. 'I could hardly believe my eyes and ears. Even when I told her that she was sending her child to an early grave, she didn't seem to get it. Astonishing.'

In such instances, you can completely understand the children for throwing a strop. Under normal scuba circumstances though, no matter what the situation is, it is best to try to hang on to your cool. The last thing any of us needs is extra anger hormones charging around our bodies at times when clear calm thinking is the order of the day. I have always remembered a story told by Thierry, a legend in his own post-dive cappuccino time at La Pirogue. He recalled how, on arriving at a dive centre in the Red Sea minus his log book, he, without hesitation, agreed to do a 'refresher' dive to show that he could do what he said he could.

Thierry probably has around 10,000 dives to his name but rather than kick up a fuss and quote his dive quota, he humbly took to the pool to show them his skills. 'Of course I didn't mind,' he replied, when a fellow coffee drinker asked the question, 'the rules are the rules.' And since the rules also say that you have to do a refresher if you haven't logged a dive within the past year, there is no point in getting uppity about being asked to do so before taking to the seas. If you see someone kicking off about it then you may have come across a know-it-all. Don't let them get to you or throw your confidence or your desire to adhere to the rules off track.

Crying underwater

This confidence-draining happened to me once when I was buddied up with a strong-willed instructor who was a stranger to the area in which we were diving. She proved to me one thing: that you can cry underwater into your regulator. So insistent was she to dive her dive rather than the planned dive that I began to stress as we went further and further away from the main group. Being a novice and thinking I was with someone responsible, I meekly followed. Big mistake. When I tried to get her to turn back, she virtually signed at me to 'sling my hook'. Tears welled up and to my surprise, there I was, having a good old blub underwater, which turned out to be no bad thing, because there is nothing like a sob to clear the tension and your mind.

I rapidly finned back to the group and left her to it. The leader of our dive had to then take the decision as to what to do. Leave us lot or leave her. He chose the latter. She realised what was happening and eventually deigned to rejoin the group. Back on dry land, he spoke to her about her lack of respect. She cancelled all her other booked dives, but that was probably a good thing for everyone concerned. I, for one, would have point-blank refused to accompany her again, but it did drum home the message that experience can lead to cockiness and *that* (sorry to go on about it but it is important) can lead to accidents.

Choosing a dive centre

Likewise, if you do not feel a sense of confidence in any unfamiliar instructor or dive centre you approach while on holiday, personally I wouldn't take the chance of diving with them either. Making the wrong choice really scuppered my brother's first scuba experience, and so far he has not plucked up the courage to have another go. It was at a diving centre while on holiday, which, unfortunately for him, on that particular day had a large group learning session with absolute beginners. 'The instructor had 16 of us diving "first timers" in the water and basically expected us to just go underwater as happy as Larry and not to have any problems. Some people were fine but some, including me, were really anxious and were spluttering and coughing all over the place,' explained Sean. He felt that the centre couldn't have cared less. They'd paid their money and it was their problem if they didn't 'get it'. 'I was really gutted. I wanted to learn to dive with my son but I honestly just got too freaked out by the whole thing. I'd like to try again, with a one-to-one lesson, but who knows?'

Making sure that the centre you choose is affiliated to a reputable diving teaching association is an important first step to help avoid these situations. So too is simply taking a look at how they do things. I think that it is well worth chatting to others who have learnt at the same centre. See what they say. It's worth doing your homework over this, as Mat and Maz told me the first time I met them at Sun Divers. 'We trawled around doing try dives at several places. When we came here we just felt as though we fitted in. And we were right, we did, and we got an excellent training. It was too important a decision to get wrong, because we are going on to teach others in our turn and we want to be able to do things the right way, the safe way.' This pretty much sums things up. If you do things the right way, the safe way, if you follow the rules, listen to those who know, and always dive within your personal limits then you can open up your life to a world so rich in wonder and fun that you just won't be able to resist doing it again. Go on, try going down. I reckon that you may just love it.

WHERE TO LEARN TO DIVE

There are many international organisations with which you can learn to dive; for a full checklist see www.subaqua.co.uk/organisations/training.shtml. Below is a brief overview of some of the better known ones, which you can contact to find out more about learning to dive recreationally.

PADI (Professional Association of Diving Instructors)
The PADI website has up-to-date dive information and caters for all your diving needs. You can find your local dive centre or resorts around the world; places at which you can take the full range of PADI courses, which take you from beginner to instructor level. To choose a place to learn to dive and to get weekly dive-related news and a monthly email newsletter, log on to **www.padi.com**.

BSAC (British Sub-Aqua Club)
A BSAC branch is a local diving club, which is affiliated with BSAC and which follows its training and qualification system. You usually learn over a number of weeks in the UK at weekly training sessions, and courses can take you from beginner to instructor level. For more information, check out **www.bsac.com.**

CMAS (Confédération Mondiale des Activités Subaquatiques)
Courses given by CMAS-trained dive instructors are found

worldwide in holiday resorts. The courses guarantee a professional and safe way to learn to dive away from British waters. Courses can take you from beginner to instructor level. See **www.cmas2000.org** for details.

Other excellent recreational dive training organisations include:

NAUI (National Association of Underwater Instructors)
UK-based. See **www.naui.org** for information.

SSI (Scuba Schools International)
See **www.divessi.com** for information.

SSAC (Scottish Sub-Aqua Club)
See **www.scotsac.com** for information.

SAA (Sub-Aqua Association)
UK-based. See **www.saa.org.uk** for information.

CFT (Comhairle Fo-Thuinn, the Irish Underwater Council)
Ireland-based. See **www.scubaireland.com** for information.

Acknowledgements

My heartfelt thanks go to Jo Hemmings at New Holland for having the sense of humour / courage (I'm not sure which or if it's both!) to take this book on. To Kate Parker for being the most bubbly, fun and lovely editor any author could wish to work with; and to Liz O'Donnell, my copy editor, for all of her hard work. To Geraldine Woods, my agent: thank you, this is our first book together so fingers crossed. To Stephen Warren at Maverick Diving for reading the manuscript. To everyone at Sun Divers, including Thierry, Bibi, Jean-Marc, Giovanni, Ken, Kaleal, Soonan, Ti-Ti, and to James and Jeewan at La Pirogue bar for always coming up with the post-dive cappuccinos and a big smile. And of course to Gérald (www.geraldrambert.com), without whom I'd still be warbling on saying 'scuba diving, me? You cannot be serious.' Thank you for opening my eyes to your underwater world and sharing it with me. It is truly beautiful. Never stop taking the photos.